Wiley Global Finance is a market-leading provider of over 400 annual books, mobile applications, elearning products, workflow training tools, newsletters and websites for both professionals and consumers in institutional finance, trading, corporate accounting, exam preparation, investing, and performance management.

www.wileyglobalfinance.com  WILEY Global Finance
WHERE DATA FINDS DIRECTION

Fisher Investments
on Financials

FISHER INVESTMENTS PRESS

Fisher Investments Press brings the research, analysis and market intelligence of Fisher Investments' research team, headed by CEO and *New York Times* best-selling author Ken Fisher, to all investors. The Press covers a range of investing and market-related topics for a wide audience—from novices to enthusiasts to professionals.

Books by Ken Fisher
Debunkery
How to Smell a Rat
Markets Never Forget (But People Do)
The Ten Roads to Riches
The Only Three Questions That Still Count
100 Minds That Made the Market
The Wall Street Waltz
Super Stocks

Fisher Investments On Series
Fisher Investments on Energy
Fisher Investments on Materials
Fisher Investments on Consumer Staples
Fisher Investments on Industrials
Fisher Investments on Emerging Markets
Fisher Investments on Consumer Discretionary
Fisher Investments on Utilities
Fisher Investments on Health Care
Fisher Investments on Technology
Fisher Investments on Telecom

Other Books by Fisher Investments Press
Own the World by Aaron Anderson
20/20 Money by Michael Hanson

FISHER
INVESTMENTS
PRESS

Fisher Investments on Financials

Fisher Investments

with

Jarred J. Kriz

WILEY

John Wiley & Sons, Inc.

Published by John Wiley & Sons, Inc., Hoboken, New Jersey.
Published simultaneously in Canada.

Important Disclaimers: This book reflects personal opinions, viewpoints and analyses of the authors and should not be regarded as a description of advisory services provided by Fisher Investments or performance returns of any Fisher Investments client. Fisher Investments manages its clients' accounts using a variety of investment techniques and strategies not necessarily discussed in this book. Nothing in this book constitutes investment advice or any recommendation with respect to a particular country, sector, industry, security or portfolio of securities. All information is impersonal and not tailored to the circumstances or investment needs of any specific person.

Limit of Liability/Disclaimer of Warranty: While the publisher and author have used their best efforts in preparing this book, they make no representations or warranties with respect to the accuracy or completeness of the contents of this book and specifically disclaim any implied warranties of merchantability or fitness for a particular purpose. No warranty may be created or extended by sales representatives or written sales materials. The advice and strategies contained herein may not be suitable for your situation. You should consult with a professional where appropriate. Neither the publisher nor author shall be liable for any loss of profit or any other commercial damages, including but not limited to special, incidental, consequential, or other damages.

For general information on our other products and services or for technical support, please contact our Customer Care Department within the United States at (800) 762-2974, outside the United States at (317) 572-3993 or fax (317) 572-4002.

Wiley also publishes its books in a variety of electronic formats. Some content that appears in print may not be available in electronic books. For more information about Wiley products, visit our web site at www.wiley.com.

Library of Congress Cataloging-in-Publication Data:

    Fisher Investments on financials/Fisher Investments; with Jarred J. Kriz.
       pages cm.—(Fisher Investments on)
    Includes index.
    ISBN 978-0-470-52706-1; ISBN 978-1-118-22037-5 (ebk);
    ISBN 978-1-118-23401-3 (ebk); ISBN 978-1-118-25871-2 (ebk)
       1. Financial services industry.   2. Finance.   3. Investments.   I. Kriz, Jarred J.
    II. Fisher Investments.
    HG173.F54   2012
    332.—dc23

                                                2012016761

Printed in the United States of America

10 9 8 7 6 5 4 3 2 1

Contents

Foreword   ix

Preface   xi

Acknowledgments   xv

Part I   Introduction   **1**

Chapter 1   Financials Basics   3

    Financials 101   4

    Financials Sector Breakdown   23

Part II   Industry Group Details   **31**

Chapter 2   Banks   33

    Banks 101   34

    Types of Banks   45

    Banks Industry Group Characteristics   48

    Bank Regulation   53

Chapter 3   Diversified Financials   63

    Capital Markets   64

    Consumer Finance   76

    Diversified Financial Services   80

Chapter 4 Insurance Industry Group   83

   Characteristics of Insurers   84

   How Do Insurance Companies Make Money?   89

   How Do Insurance Companies Act?   94

   Regulation   98

Chapter 5 Real Estate Industry Group   103

   What Is a REIT?   105

   REIT Characteristics   108

   A Representative Example: Annaly
   Capital Management   112

   Equity REIT Sub-Industries   115

   Unique Measurements for REITs   118

Part III   Thinking Like a Portfolio Manager   121

Chapter 6 The Top-Down Method   123

   Investing Is a Science   123

   The Top-Down Method   126

   Top-Down Deconstructed   131

   Managing Against a Financials Benchmark   139

Chapter 7 Security Analysis   143

   Make Your Selection   144

   A Five-Step Process   145

   Financials Analysis   153

Chapter 8 Financials Investing Strategies   159

   Adding Value at the Sector Level   160

   Adding Value at the Country or Industry Level   161

   Adding Value at the Security Level   162

Appendix A: Reference Material   165

Appendix B: Derivatives   171

Appendix C: Risk-Adjusted Balance Sheet   175

Notes   179

About the Author   185

Index   187

Foreword

I'm pleased to introduce the eleventh in a series of investing guides from Fisher Investments Press. This imprint—the first ever from a money manager—was launched in partnership with John Wiley & Sons to bring whatever my firm can in the way of educational materials to you, whether you're an investing enthusiast, student or aspiring professional.

With this book on Financials, we've completed the 10 standard investing sectors (Energy, Materials, Consumer Staples, Health Care, Utilities, etc.) and 1 book on a region (Emerging Markets). Each book is intended to stand alone—read one or just a few on topics that interest you. However, if you like this one, you now have access to a full complement of sector investing guides—a comprehensive, do-it-yourself training program for capital markets analysis—from the comfort of your couch.

Financials may conjure bad feelings in some readers. After all, the big 2008 bear market was Financials-led and the accompanying recession particularly deep. But this book isn't merely a retread of the primary causes and outcome of that episode—such a focus would be too narrow and wouldn't help you shape forward-looking expectations for the sector.

Nor are Financials inherently bad. In fact, Financials firms are critical to the very functioning of healthy capital markets. All sectors, including Financials, have periods they lead and others they lag—sometimes badly. Individual sectors do occasionally fall big—but not forever. Over long periods, finance theory says all well-constructed equity categories (like sectors) should yield relatively similar returns, though traveling different paths.

And the "different paths" is where this book comes in. Your aim, as an investor, is to understand what drives a sector and its industries, and what makes it more likely for investors to bid stock prices up or down over the next 12 to 24 months.

For example, Financials firms can be particularly sensitive to new regulation. But how? They are also sensitive to interest rate moves— some industries more so than others. Which? And how do interest rates affect them? The book shows you. Financials, as I write, is the biggest standard sector (at 19% of the MSCI World Index) and is fully global—so any analysis must also include an understanding of global regulatory issues, interest rates, liquidity, securities demand and other key issues. A US-only focus can mean missing major factors that can drive the sector up or down. The book will walk you through how to understand global drivers and how to shape forward-looking expectations, no matter the market environment.

Don't expect to get tips on hot stocks or a "formula" or secret code for finding them. In my third of a century-plus investing money for private clients and big institutions, I've never run across such a thing. Rather, this book provides a workable, repeatable framework for increasing the likelihood of finding profitable opportunities in the Financials sector as well as managing risk. And the good news is the investing methodology presented here works for all investing sectors and the broader market. This methodology should serve you not only this year or next, but the whole of your investing career. So good luck, and enjoy the journey.

Ken Fisher
CEO of Fisher Investments

Preface

The *Fisher Investments On* series is designed to provide individual investors, students and aspiring investment professionals the tools necessary to understand and analyze investment opportunities, primarily for investing in global stocks.

Within the framework of a "top-down" investment method (more on that in Chapter 6), each guide is an easily accessible primer to economic sectors, regions or other components of the global stock market. While this guide is specifically on Financials, the basic investment methodology is applicable for analyzing any global sector, regardless of the current macroeconomic environment.

Why a top-down method? Vast evidence shows high-level, or "macro," investment decisions are ultimately more important portfolio performance drivers than individual stocks. In other words, before picking stocks, investors can benefit greatly by first deciding if stocks are the best investment relative to other assets (like bonds or cash) and then choosing categories of stocks most likely to perform best on a forward-looking basis.

For example, a Financials sector stock picker probably did pretty well from 2003 to 2006—real estate trends were mostly favorable and lending robust. However, his picks did extraordinarily poorly in 2007 and 2008 as conditions reversed and financial panic ultimately set in. Was he just smarter earlier in the decade? Did his analysis turn bad somehow? Unlikely. What mattered most was stocks in general (and especially Financials stocks) did relatively well from 2003 to early 2006 and very poorly in 2007 and 2008. In other words, a top-down perspective on the broader economy was key to navigating markets— stock picking just wasn't as important.

Fisher Investments on Financials will guide you in making top-down investment decisions specifically for the Financials sector. It shows how to determine better times to invest in Financials, what Financials industries are likelier to do best and how individual stocks can benefit in various environments. The global Financials sector is complex, covering many industries and countries with unique characteristics. Using our framework, you will be better equipped to identify their differences, spot opportunities and avoid major pitfalls.

This book takes a global approach to Financials investing. Most US investors typically invest the majority of their assets in domestic securities; they forget America is less than half of the world stock market by weight—over 50% of investment opportunities are outside our borders. This is even more important in the Financials sector because a larger proportion of the world's Financials weight is based outside the US. Given the vast market landscape and diverse geographic operations, it's vital to have a global perspective when investing in Financials today.

USING YOUR FINANCIALS GUIDE

This guide is designed in three parts. The introduction, Chapter 1, discusses vital sector basics, including the nature of the sector, its makeup and some core characteristics.

Part II, "Industry Group Details," walks through the next step of sector analysis. Each of the four chapters will focus on one of the four industry groups. Here, we'll take you through the global Financials sector investment universe and its diverse components. The Financials sector itself includes 4 industry groups, 8 industries and 26 sub-industries. Various firms are driven by enterprise spending, others by consumers and some by real estate trends. Many are leveraged to combinations of these, yet others are leveraged to none. We will take you through the industries in detail, how they operate and what drives profitability—to give you the tools to determine which industry will most likely outperform or underperform looking forward.

Part III, "Thinking Like a Portfolio Manager," delves into a top-down investment methodology and individual security analysis. You'll learn to ask important questions like: What are the most important elements to consider when analyzing property and casualty or commercial banking firms? What are the greatest risks and red flags? This book gives you a five-step process to help differentiate firms so you can identify ones with a greater probability of outperforming. We'll also discuss a few investment strategies to help determine when and how to overweight specific industries within the sector.

Fisher Investments on Financials won't give you a "silver bullet" for picking the right Financials stocks. The fact is the "right" Financials stocks will be different in different times and situations. Instead, this guide provides a framework for understanding the sector and its industries so you can be dynamic and find information the market hasn't yet priced in. There won't be any stock recommendations, target prices, political stances or even a suggestion of whether now is a good time to be invested in the Financials sector. The goal is to provide you with tools to make these decisions for yourself, now and in the future. Ultimately, our aim is to give you the framework for repeated, successful investing. Enjoy.

Acknowledgments

A number of colleagues and friends deserve tremendous praise and thanks for helping make this book a reality. We would like to extend our immense gratitude to Ken Fisher for providing the opportunity to write this book. Jeff Silk deserves our thanks for constantly challenging us to improve and presenting new and insightful questions as fast as we can answer them. Our colleagues at Fisher Investments also deserve enormous thanks for continually sharing their wealth of knowledge, insights and analysis. Without these people, the very concept of this book would never have been possible.

We owe a huge debt of gratitude to Lara Hoffmans, Michael Hanson and Aaron Anderson, without whose guidance, patience and editing contributions this book would not have been completed. A big thanks is also due to William Glaser and Andrew Teufel—aside from making this book a possibility, both are core architects of much of the thought process herein. Amanda Williams helped make the book shorter—and clearer—with some heavy-lifting content editing and eagle-eyed copy-editing. Leila Amiri designed the terrific looking cover. A special thanks to Michael Kelly, Richard Bueche, Akash Patel, Charles Thies and Brian Kepp for contributing content, putting up with endless questions and offering their insightful opinions. We'd also like to thank Alex Nelson and the rest of Roger Bohl's team of research associates for their help tracking down and formatting elusive data. Marc Haberman, Molly Lienesch and Fabrizio Ornani were also instrumental in the creation of Fisher Investments Press, which created the infrastructure behind this book. We'd also like to thank our team at Wiley for their support and guidance throughout this project, especially Laura Walsh.

Jarred Kriz would also like to specifically thank his wife, Dawn, for her love, understanding, patience and encouragement.

Fisher Investments
on Financials

INTRODUCTION

I

1

FINANCIALS BASICS

Trends within the Financials sector are often topics of heated debate, and for good reason—not only is it the largest sector in most broad equity indexes globally, but it revolves around one of the things most hold very dear: money. Money is transferred, multiplied, protected and placed at risk in the Financials sector. The sector is considered the lifeblood of the global economy—and while a properly working Financials sector can be a boon, its going haywire can have unfortunate consequences.

Many of this sector's products and services are relatively simple, like making a cash deposit at a bank or using a charge card for your morning cup of coffee. And many are quite complex, like making a leveraged bet in a synthetic collateralized debt obligation. Financial innovation has transformed the sector from its simple roots into an incredibly complex system—so complex that, at times, it can engender great fear.

Globally, governments are well aware of the complexity and importance of the Financials sector, making it one of the world's most highly regulated sectors. From central banks to financial services authorities to consumer protection agencies—the government's hand in the

Financials sector is a core concern, capable of promoting prosperity or driving disaster in the sector and economy as a whole.

This book's intention is not to provide detailed instruction on complex financial structures' construction, focus on the 2008 financial panic (as many other books attempt to do) or discuss in detail the impact of myriad proposed and existing regulations, but rather to help readers make better decisions about when to over- or underweight the sector (or the industry positioning within) as part of an overall portfolio strategy. Moreover, we attempt to demystify many of the sector's complexities and allow for a better understanding of trends. The aim is not to provide definitive answers, but to help readers learn to think critically about this and, indeed, any other sector.

Global Versus Domestic

In our view, a global approach to investing is superior to a domestic-only approach because it allows for greater diversification and more opportunity. However, for data availability, consistency and reliability reasons, we often use domestic data to demonstrate a point. Most often, we refer to the S&P 500 for domestic trends and either the MSCI World or MSCI All Country World Index (ACWI) for global trends. The S&P 500 is an index of the largest US firms, the MSCI World represents the largest developed world firms and the MSCI ACWI also includes Emerging Markets.

FINANCIALS 101

The Financials sector is quite a bit more diverse than many who are new to analysis might assume. However, at a very high level, there are some overarching defining characteristics. First and foremost, it is, as of this writing, the world's largest sector. In addition, the sector tends to be:

- A relatively more volatile sector that tracks closely with broader markets
- More "value" oriented than "growth"

- Neither big nor small
- Sensitive to interest rates
- Not cyclical, yet not defensive
- Heavily regulated
- Highly leveraged and reliant on other people's money (OPM)

The Largest Sector

The Financials sector is the largest in most global and country-specific benchmarks simply because it represents more companies with more assets, income, equity and sales than any other sector.

Balance Sheets In terms of assets and shareholder equity—two main components of any company's balance sheet—the Financials sector accounts for $89 trillion in assets and nearly $7 trillion in equity.[1] That's 72% of assets of all firms in the MSCI All Country World Index and 32% of all shareholder equity (see Table 1.1).[2] Simply put, the Financials sector dwarfs all others.

Definitions: Assets and Shareholder Equity

Assets are items of economic value that can be converted to cash, like equipment, securities or real estate. To many financial companies, loans or securities tied to loans are core assets.

Shareholder equity, also known as net worth, is equal to assets minus liabilities.

Income Statements Using the income statement to value a company is a common technique. Often, a company will be valued based on a multiple of its total sales or net income. When it comes to Financials sector firms, both measurements are often used. Each illustrates the sector's size, but to a lesser degree than assets or equity (as shown in Table 1.2).

Comparing the balance sheets and income statements of companies within the broad market, the Financials sector's large weight

Table 1.1   Percent of Assets and Shareholder Equity by Sector

MSCI ACWI Sector	Assets	Equity
Financials	72%	32%
Industrials	5%	9%
Consumer Discretionary	4%	9%
Energy	4%	14%
Utilities	3%	6%
Materials	3%	8%
Telecommunication Services	2%	6%
Consumer Staples	2%	6%
Information Technology	2%	6%
Health Care	2%	5%

Source: Thomson Reuters; MSCI, Inc.,[3] as of 12/31/2010.

Table 1.2   Percent of Aggregate Sales and Net Income by Sector (2004–2010)

MSCI ACWI Sector	Sales	Income
Financials	17%	22%
Energy	16%	16%
Industrials	13%	10%
Materials	13%	10%
Consumer Staples	11%	8%
Consumer Discretionary	7%	8%
Health Care	6%	8%
Information Technology	6%	7%
Telecommunication Services	6%	6%
Utilities	5%	5%

Source: Thomson Reuters; MSCI, Inc.,[4] as of 12/31/2010.

seems reasonable. In fact, with the sector accounting for 22% of net income and 32% of equity, it is easy to understand why the Financials sector plays such a prominent role in most broad equity market indexes.[5]

Financials Sector Weight

Thanks to financial innovation, increased credit penetration and growing acceptance of debt, the Financials sector has more than doubled its weight in the S&P 500 over the last 20 years (see Table 1.3). This trend illustrates the US economy's transition from an industrial economy to a more information- or knowledge-based economy. But it's not just in the US. Globally, knowledge-based sectors like Technology and Financials have grown, while Industrial and Manufacturing sectors have shrunk. The difference is more pronounced in developed economies since many emerging economies remain more dependent on raw materials and manufacturing.

A More Volatile Sector

The Financials sector tends to be more volatile on average than others yet also tracks closely with broader markets. From 12/31/1974 to 12/31/2011 (a period for which we have good sector data), the Financials sector returned a 9.6% annualized average compared to the S&P 500's 11.5%.[6]

Don't take that to mean Financials is a below-average sector. No— all well-constructed categories of stocks should yield similar returns over very long time periods. There's no fundamental reason one category should be any better or worse than any other—though they will all go through periods of leading or lagging. For example, from 12/31/1974 to

Table 1.3 Financial S&P 500 Weights Since 1990

S&P 500	1990	1995	2010	2011
Financials Weight in Index	**7.1%**	**12.7%**	**16.5%**	**14.3%**
Banks	40%	53%	42%	35%
Real Estate Investment & Services	0%	0%	0%	1%
Real Estate Investment Trusts	1%	0%	8%	13%
Life Insurance	8%	5%	7%	7%
Nonlife Insurance	31%	20%	16%	18%
Financial Services (Sector)	21%	21%	26%	27%

Source: Thomson Reuters; ICB Classifications; S&P 500 Index from 12/31/1990 to 12/31/2011.

12/31/2007 (before 2008's financial crisis), the sector was in line with the S&P 500. Its poorer relative average return now is due to the pretty steep Financials sector-led bear market in the late 2000s.

A relative return index is an easy way to plot the trend of two data series' relative performance over time. In Figure 1.1, the gray line represents the value of the S&P 500 Financials index divided by the value of the S&P 500 index, while the arrows show general directional trends. As the Financials index outperforms the S&P 500 index, the line moves higher, and vice versa.

Most major stints of relative under- or outperformance have been *event driven*—meaning some major, largely unanticipated event shocked the system some way and changed the sector's relative trajectory. (Again, see Figure 1.1.) After fairly in-line performance from the 1970s to mid-1980s, the sector underperformed through the early 1990s as the Savings & Loan (S&L) crisis (as well as multiple sector-specific issues) weighed on it. Outperformance from the early 1990s to the late 1990s was tied to attractive valuations, innovation and a generally

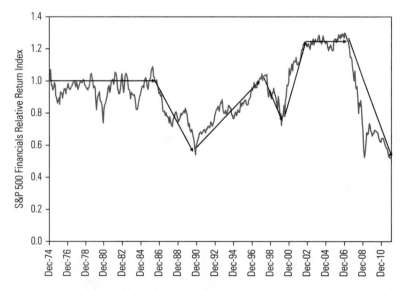

Figure 1.1   S&P 500 Financials Sector Relative Return Index

Source: Global Financial Data, Inc.; S&P 500 Financials Sector versus S&P 500 Index from 12/31/2004 to 12/31/2011.

stable economic environment. Long Term Capital Management, the Asian Contagion and the tech/Internet boom drove Financials sector underperformance into 2000—until the "new economy" blew up and Financials performed well since the sector was relatively insulated from the Internet debacle. Investors moved to value investing, and real estate trends buoyed bank credit quality. In the late 2000s, however, the sector vastly underperformed tied to increased losses from souring mortgage loans, which intensified as a financial panic arose.

Globally, the trend is similar except for a stark difference during the late 1980s and early 1990s: While US Financials was plagued with domestic issues such as the S&L crisis and bad oil sector loans, foreign Financials was not. As a result, foreign Financials outperformed during the late 1980s. Conversely, as domestic Financials recovered in the early 1990s, foreign Financials was pressured as US financial companies re-emerged on the global scene and competition increased. Trends between US and foreign Financials in the 1970s, early 1980s and from the mid-1990s to early 2000s are similar, but since foreign Financials did not suffer through the late 1980s, it has outperformed domestic Financials since 1974.

While sector returns over long periods of time are similar, each sector does vary in its return volatility. One common measure of volatility is *standard deviation.*

Standard Deviation

Standard deviation measures the historic deviation from average returns over time. The higher the standard deviation, the higher the swings in returns during any given time period.

There are three levels of deviation. A one-standard deviation event demonstrates events within a 64.2% probability band. A two-standard deviation event demonstrates events outside the 64.2% probability band. A three-standard deviation event is something that doesn't happen 99.6% of the time. When given the standard deviation of returns, this number typically illustrates a one-standard deviation event—meaning if the sector's standard deviation is 23.3% returns will vary from 23.3% above to 23.3% below its average return over time with a 64.2% probability.

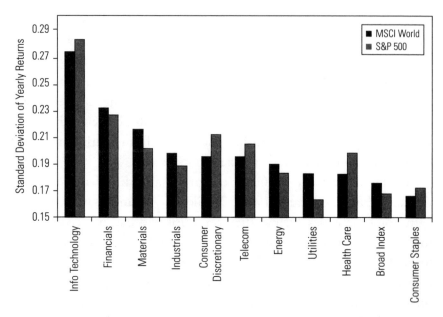

Figure 1.2   MSCI World and S&P 500 Sector Standard Deviation of Yearly Returns

Source: Global Financial Data, Inc.; Thomson Reuters; MSCI World Sector Indexes and S&P 500 Sector Indexes, Rolling 12-Month Returns from 12/31/1974 to 12/31/2011.

The Financials sector globally and domestically has the second highest standard deviation of returns over time, just behind the Information Technology sector (see Figure 1.2). Even stripping out the unusually high volatility associated with 2008's financial panic and the subsequent sovereign debt crisis, Financials still remains the second most volatile sector by this measure.

So, Financials is typically more volatile than the market average—but that doesn't mean it widely deviates from the broad market direction. Remember, a rising tide lifts most boats. When broad markets rise, so do Financials—usually. And when markets fall, so do Financials—most of the time. However, because of Financials' exposure to capital markets–related functions—like asset management, brokerage and investment banking—and its high leverage, which amplifies gains and losses, it tends to be sensitive to overall market trends (i.e., it has a relatively high *beta*).

Beta, Correlation and R-Squared

Beta is a measurement of how responsive a financial asset is to the market as a whole. An asset with a beta of 1.1 is expected to perform roughly 10% better than the market in a rising market and 10% worse in a falling market.

Correlation is a statistical measure of how two securities move in relation to each other. The measurement, or coefficient, ranges between 1 and −1, with 1 being a perfectly positive relationship and −1 being perfectly negative. R-squared is calculated by squaring the correlation coefficient and represents the explanatory relationship between two securities. In other words, when compared to the S&P 500, a stock with a correlation coefficient of 0.80 would have an R-squared of 0.64, which means 64% of its movement can be generally explained by the S&P 500's movement.

The S&P 500 Financials sector has a beta of 1.10, and the MSCI World Financials Index has a beta of 1.18, relative to the respective broad market indexes, since 1974.[7] This makes it the highest beta sector globally and third highest domestically. (See Table 1.4.) Typically, a higher historical beta is indicative of a sector that is more economically sensitive over time—sectors like Technology, Financials and Consumer Discretionary fit the bill. A beta greater than 1 tells us the sector typically goes up more than the market in up markets and

Table 1.4   Sector Beta

	MSCI World	S&P 500
Financials	**1.18**	**1.10**
Information Technology	1.13	1.35
Industrials	1.05	1.04
Consumer Discretionary	1.03	1.11
Telecom	0.80	0.86
Utilities	0.79	0.62
Health Care	0.76	0.85
Energy	0.72	0.71
Consumer Staples	0.69	0.67

Source: Global Financial Data, Inc.; Thomson Reuters from 12/31/1974 to 12/31/2011.

down more in down markets—but this relationship is not static, as you can see in Figure 1.3.

The Financials sector is also highly correlated to the broader market. (See Table 1.5.) This is not so surprising since at 20% to 30%

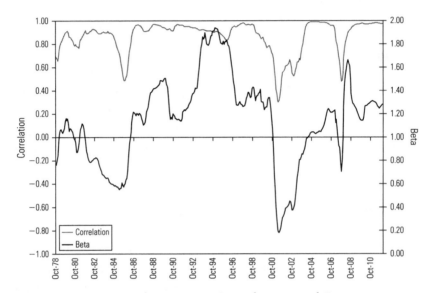

Figure 1.3   Financials Sector's Correlation and Beta
Source: Global Financial Data, Inc., 36-month rolling correlation and beta from 12/31/1947 to 12/31/2011.

Table 1.5   Sector Correlation

	MSCI World	S&P 500
Industrials	0.93	0.92
Consumer Discretionary	0.93	0.87
Financials	**0.90**	**0.82**
Materials	0.83	0.77
Utilities	0.76	0.64
Consumer Staples	0.73	0.65
Health Care	0.73	0.72
Information Technology	0.73	0.80
Telecom	0.72	0.71
Energy	0.67	0.65

Source: Global Financial Data, Inc.; Thomson Reuters, as of 12/31/2010.

of most broad market indexes, it contributes a large portion to broad market returns.

As with other sectors, the Financials sector beta and broader market correlation ebb and flow over time. Sometimes, like during the 2008 credit panic, the sector's beta is higher than normal. And other times, like the early 2000s Technology-led bear market, beta was lower as Financials considerably outperformed in an overall falling market. The correlation of the sector is usually highly positive, but again, it varies over time, just like the other sectors. Figure 1.3 shows Financials correlation and beta to the S&P 500 rising and falling over time.

More "Value" Than "Growth"

Financials firms tend to be more value oriented than growth. Table 1.6 shows the composition (by sector market cap) of common growth or value indexes. Financials is much more prevalent in the value index. Additionally, when looking at how much of each sector is considered value (by market cap), only Utilities and Telecom are more

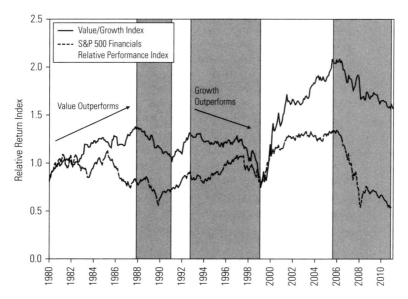

Figure 1.4   Growth Versus Value Cycles and Financials Relative Performance
Source: Thomson Reuters; Russell 3000 Index from 01/31/1979 to 12/31/2011.

Table 1.6   Sector Weights in Growth and Value Indexes

MSCI AC Sector	Value	Growth
Financials	**30%**	**9%**
Energy	15%	8%
Health Care	10%	8%
Industrials	8%	13%
Telecommunication Services	7%	2%
Materials	6%	9%
Consumer Discretionary	6%	15%
Utilities	6%	1%
Consumer Staples	6%	15%
Information Technology	5%	20%

Source: Thomson Reuters, as of 12/31/2011.

value-centric. Conversely (and not surprisingly), Tech is the most growth-oriented sector. As a result of Financials' value-ish nature, the sector has a 30% weight in the MSCI ACWI Value index but just 9% in the Growth index.[8]

What Is Value? And What Is Growth?

Firms deemed to have a relatively low price compared to some metric or set of metrics such as cash flow or book value, or those that have low earnings growth or high dividend yields, are usually called "value" firms—i.e., they're a good value for the price.

Firms positioned opposite to value firms, such as those with high earnings growth and perhaps low dividends, are considered "growth." The idea is investors are willing to pay a higher price in anticipation of those metrics growing—earnings rocketing up, the enterprise growing in value, etc.

Some investors prefer value stocks, while others favor growth. Over long periods, neither group has very different performance, and neither is inherently superior to the other.

Like all major categories, value and growth trade leadership in irregular cycles. From 1979 to 2005, there were four distinct growth cycles and three prolonged value cycles, with many shorter cycles within the longer cycles. Since Financials is more value than growth, Financials typically underperforms during growth cycles and outperforms during value cycles. Figure 1.4 shows periods when growth (gray area) or value (white area) is generally outperforming the broader market. Note how Financials' relative performance tends to act similarly to, though not exactly like, the value/growth index.

Highly Leveraged

More than firms in any other sector, Financials firms tend to be highly *leveraged*—meaning they have a lot of liabilities on their books relative to equity. (See Table 1.7.) A simple way to measure leverage is to examine a basic assets-to-equity ratio (assets/equity). Because its firms are so leveraged, changes in asset values have a much larger impact on the Financials sector than on any other.

Table 1.7   Leverage Ratio by Sector (MSCI AC World Sectors)

	Leverage Ratio
Financials	**13.8**
Banks	**17.0**
Insurance	**11.5**
Real Estate	**2.4**
Diversified Financials	**12.9**
Industrials	3.5
Utilities	3.4
Consumer Discretionary	3.0
Telecommunication Services	2.6
Consumer Staples	2.5
Materials	2.2
Health Care	2.2
Information Technology	2.1
Energy	2.0

Source: Thomson Reuters; MSCI, Inc.,[9] as of 12/31/2011.

Among Financials sector sub-industries, Banks are the most leveraged based on a basic assets/equity ratio. However, bank leverage is wildly complex, and though a basic leverage ratio can be used for simple comparison purposes, it does not show the whole picture. Many other types of leverage ratios are utilized in the group, which can lower the stated leverage if asset values are altered by risk-weighting certain assets or accounting for collateral. (More on this in Chapter 2.)

Interest Rate Sensitivity

All sectors are sensitive to interest rate trends in some way. However, since Financials firms are, by definition, heavily exposed to financial assets and are typically leveraged to boot, interest rate trends tend to be more important.

From 1990 to 2010, Financials sector income growth had an R-squared of 0.62 to the 10-year US Treasury bond yield, while collectively, non-Financials sectors had an R-squared of 0.40. Additionally, relative to the US Federal Funds Target Rate (short-term interest rate) over the same period, the Financials sector's income growth had a 0.31 R-squared versus 0.10 in non-Financials sectors.[10]

In the stock market, the 10-year yield has a similar impact—most of the time. Since 1970, the Financials sector's relative performance has been highly negatively correlated to the 10-year yield except during certain stressed periods—the credit panic, recession and recovery of the late 2000s, the Asian Contagion in the late 1990s and the extraordinarily high interest rates of the early 1980s. (See Figure 1.5.)

Companies within the Financials sector are impacted by interest rates in many ways. Since interest rates simply represent the cost of borrowing, higher interest rates make borrowing more expensive, while lower interest rates make borrowing cheaper and promote loan growth. Insurance companies prefer higher interest rates so their investment portfolios earn more interest income. Real estate companies find higher interest rates troublesome because they can pressure real estate portfolio values, while investment banks and brokers prefer higher rates to capture higher spreads.

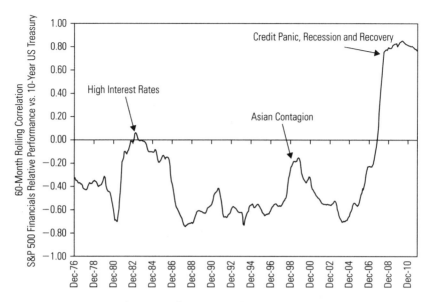

Figure 1.5   Correlation of Financials Sector Relative Performance and Interest Rates

Source: Global Financial Data, Inc.; S&P 500 Financials and S&P 500 Indexes; Federal Reserve 10-Year US Treasury Yield from December 1975 to December 2011.

Since the sector is dominated by lenders, trends therein drive the sector's relationship with interest rates for the most part, and Financials stocks tend to do a bit better when interest rates are falling as investors anticipate greater profits from greater volumes. Conversely, Financials stocks tend to underperform in rising interest rate environments. (We will go into more detail on how interest rates impact the various industries in subsequent chapters.)

Since 1970, there have been 10 distinct periods of rising interest rates (see Table 1.8). US Financials underperformed in all but four, with average annual underperformance (relative to the S&P 500) of –2.9%.[11] Falling interest rates are typically less bad for Financials over time—Financials underperform by –0.4%[12] which isn't immaterial, but much of the underperformance can be attributed to poor relative performance leading up to and following the 2008 financial panic. Nothing is absolute in investing—Financials can outperform in a

Table 1.8   Financials Relative Performance and Interest Rates

Rising 10-Year Interest Rates

Begin	End	S&P 500 Financials	S&P 500	Relative	Change in 10y Yield (bps)
12/31/1970	9/30/1975	−1%	8%	−8%	198
12/31/1976	9/30/1981	38%	37%	1%	903
5/31/1983	6/30/1984	−22%	−1%	−21%	303
1/31/1987	10/31/1987	−19%	−6%	−13%	170
10/31/1993	11/30/1994	−6%	0%	−6%	248
1/31/1996	4/30/1997	44%	29%	15%	112
10/31/1998	1/31/2000	10%	29%	−19%	204
6/30/2003	6/30/2006	42%	38%	4%	161
12/31/2008	4/30/2010	32%	35%	−3%	144
10/31/2010	2/28/2011	16%	13%	3%	96
	Average	13%	18%	−5%	
	Average Annualized Return (ARR)	5%	8%	−2.9%	

Falling 10-Year Interest Rates

Begin	End	S&P 500 Financials	S&P 500	Relative	Change in 10y Yield (bps)
9/30/1975	12/31/1976	48%	34%	13%	−167
9/30/1981	5/31/1983	60%	53%	8%	−503
6/30/1984	1/31/1987	118%	97%	21%	−666
10/31/1987	10/31/1993	137%	127%	11%	−345
11/30/1994	1/31/1996	64%	44%	20%	−231
4/30/1997	10/31/1998	35%	40%	−5%	−208
1/31/2000	6/30/2003	13%	−27%	40%	−314
6/30/2006	12/31/2008	−58%	−25%	−33%	−290
4/30/2010	10/31/2010	−10%	1%	−10%	−106
2/28/2011	12/31/2011	−22%	−4%	−18%	−170
	Average	39%	34%	5%	
	ARR	11%	11%	−0.4%	

Source: Global Financial Data, Inc., from 12/31/1970 to 12/31/2011.

rising or falling interest rate environment. And, with underperformance in only 6 out of 10 periods, we can say interest rate trends are important, but many other factors also impact the sector over time.

Definition: Duration

Interest rates clearly impact the Financials sector, but they have a varying impact on assets and liabilities, depending in part on duration. Duration measures the time required to recover a dollar of price in present value terms. To fixed-income investors, such as most companies in the Financials sector, duration represents a security's interest rate sensitivity. Typically, a higher-duration security will be more sensitive to changes in interest rates.

Not Cyclical, Yet Not Defensive

Most sectors tend to favor either bull or bear markets more markedly, but the history for Financials is mixed. In that sense, Financials can't be clearly labeled as either cyclical (i.e., does better in a bull) or defensive (i.e., does better in a bear), despite the sector's cyclical underpinnings.

For many other sectors, getting a broad market call right can go a long way toward knowing whether a sector will perform reasonably well—but that may not work for Financials. Over longer periods, Financials' relative performance in both bulls and bears works out to be similar (see Tables 1.9 and 1.10, which show bull and bear markets since 1972 and relative Financials performance), but that similar relative performance comes with some major deviations. For example, Financials strongly outperformed during the great 1990s bull market. The 1990s bull market followed extreme stresses in the previous decade that were driven by geographical and sector-specific issues: Mutual savings banks in the Northeast, S&Ls nationally, agricultural banks in the Midwest, oil patch banks in the Southwest and real estate loans in coastal states—all of these hammered Financials. As these issues passed, the Financials sector was attractively valued

Table 1.9   S&P 500 Financials Versus S&P 500 Composite in Bull Markets

Bull Markets

Begin	End	S&P 500 Financials	S&P 500	Relative
9/30/1974	11/30/1980	116%	195%	**−79%**
8/31/1982	8/31/1987	192%	237%	**−45%**
12/31/1987	7/31/1990	41%	58%	**−17%**
10/31/1990	3/31/2000	792%	515%	277%
10/31/2002	10/31/2007	69%	92%	**−22%**
3/31/2009	12/31/2011	53%	67%	−14%
	Average	211%	194%	17%
	ARR	17%	18%	−1.2%

Source: Global Financial Data, Inc.; S&P 500 Indexes, from 12/31/1971 to 12/31/2011.

Table 1.10   S&P 500 Financials Versus S&P 500 Composite in Bear Markets

Bear Markets

Begin	End	S&P 500 Financials	S&P 500	Relative
12/31/1972	9/30/1974	−46%	−43%	**−3%**
11/30/1980	8/31/1982	17%	−7%	24%
8/31/1987	12/31/1987	−30%	−24%	**−6%**
7/31/1990	10/31/1990	−29%	−14%	**−15%**
3/31/2000	10/31/2002	−3%	−39%	36%
10/31/2007	3/31/2009	−72%	−47%	**−26%**
	Average	−27%	−29%	2%
	ARR	−26%	−24%	−2.8%

Source: Global Financial Data, Inc.; S&P 500 Indexes, from 12/31/1971 to 12/31/2011.

and ripe to take advantage of a growing economy, falling interest rates and stable inflation.

Then, Financials badly lagged in a 2007–2009 bear market caused primarily by issues specific to the Financials sector. Essentially, Financials' performance and market cycles do not go hand in hand, and unless you can forecast an exception—perhaps a banking crisis—it is best not to allow the market cycle to dictate your relative Financials weighting.

When it comes to economic cycles, it is a similar story—getting a broad macroeconomic call correct likely won't be enough to reliably predict forward-looking Financials outperformance. During the seven economic expansions since 1970 (see Tables 1.11 and 1.12), Financials underperformed four times. However, average annualized performance overall through the expansions was just shy of the S&P

Table 1.11   Financials Sector Relative Performance During Economic Expansions

Economic Expansion

Begin	End	S&P 500 Financials	S&P 500	Relative
12/31/70	11/30/73	33%	14%	20%
03/31/75	01/31/80	58%	71%	−13%
07/31/80	07/31/81	20%	13%	7%
11/30/82	07/31/90	116%	243%	−128%
03/31/91	03/31/01	531%	285%	247%
11/30/01	12/31/07	31%	44%	−13%
06/30/09	12/31/2011	13%	44%	−31%
	Average	115%	102%	13%
	ARR	11.9%	12.4%	−0.5%

Source: Global Financial Data, Inc.; National Bureau of Economic Research; S&P 500 Indexes Total Return from 1970 to 2011.

Table 1.12   Financials Sector Relative Performance During Economic Recessions

Economic Recession

Begin	End	S&P 500 Financials	S&P 500	Relative
11/30/73	03/31/75	−21%	−8%	−13%
01/31/80	07/31/80	6%	9%	−4%
07/31/81	11/30/82	28%	14%	14%
07/31/90	03/31/91	11%	8%	3%
03/31/01	11/30/01	−1%	−1%	0%
12/31/07	06/30/09	−57%	−35%	−22%
	Average	−6%	−2%	−4%
	ARR	−11%	−4%	−7.0%

Source: Global Financial Data, Inc.; National Bureau of Economic Research; S&P 500 Indexes Total Return from 1970 to 2011.

500 because return dispersion was material in a few periods. Of note, Financials greatly underperformed during the long 1980s expansion, thanks in no small part to the S&L crisis. Then, Financials vastly outperformed in the 1990s expansion.

During economic recessions, the sector underperforms on average, but absent the dislocations in the 2007–2009 period, performance about matches the broader market. As with market cycles, these data illustrate relative performance is often driven by one-off events like a financial panic or crisis.

Heavily Regulated

Because the financial system is the backbone of most economies, Financials is one of the (if not the) most highly regulated sectors in the world. Understanding how the sector is regulated and why are key to making better forward-looking forecasts. (We cover regulation in more depth in Chapters 2 through 5.)

Financials core regulators/overseers include:

- Committee of European Banking Supervisors
- Bank for International Settlements (Basel)
- Global central banks (US Federal Reserve, European Central Bank, Bank of Japan, Bank of England, etc.)
- Financial services authorities (FSA, ASIC, CSSF, AMF, etc.)
- Consumer Financial Protection Bureau
- Federal Deposit Insurance Corporation
- Comptroller of the Currency
- Securities and Exchange Commission
- State bank and insurance regulators

Decisions made by these (and similar) entities can greatly impact the sector. Whether tightening consumer protections (which could reduce profitability) or mandating higher capitalization levels (which could cause a painful round of dilution), regulators impact investors. However, changes are inevitable, and investors can't much control future regulation—so investors shouldn't dwell on "bad" regulation.

And wishing regulation were implemented differently is mostly fruitless. Rather, investors should attempt to decipher regulation and how new or existing rules likely impact Financials stocks' future profitability. Also, regulation often punishes some at the benefit of others—what's known as "regulatory arbitrage"—so correctly determining the likely winners and positioning portfolios accordingly can add relative value.

Reliant on Other People's Money (OPM)

The Financials sector is unique among most other sectors because a major driver is trends within capital markets. What's good for capital markets is usually good for Financials firms. For example, is the aggregate economy increasing its borrowing? Do investors have more assets to be saved, managed, hedged, brokered or exchanged? Are higher asset values driving increased need for insurance? Are higher real estate values allowing for higher rents? These questions need to be answered when considering positioning within the Financials sector, and we will discuss these further as they relate to the various industry groups in subsequent chapters.

FINANCIALS SECTOR BREAKDOWN

The Financials sector is fairly diverse, so understanding its industry groups and sub-industries is important to overall sector analysis. A useful way to understand how the sector breaks down is looking at the industry-standard GICS.

Global Industry Classification Standards (GICS)

The Global Industry Classification Standard (GICS) is a widely accepted framework for classifying companies into groups based on similarities. The GICS structure consists of 10 sectors, 24 industry groups, 68 industries and 154 sub-industries. This structure offers four levels of hierarchy:

- Sector
- Industry group

- Industry
- Sub-industry

According to GICS, the Financials sector consists of 4 industry groups, 8 industries and 26 sub-industries. The sector is one of the broadest with the most representative companies in the GICS framework, and it contains the second largest number of sub-industries, trailing the Consumer Discretionary sector. Following are the industry groups and corresponding industries for the sector.

Industry Group: Banks
- Commercial Banks
- Thrifts & Mortgage Finance

Industry Group: Diversified Financials
- Diversified Financial Services
- Consumer Finance
- Capital Markets

Industry Group: Insurance
- Insurance

Industry Group: Real Estate
- Real Estate Investment Trusts (REITs)
- Real Estate Management & Development

Chapters 2, 3, 4 and 5 delve deeper into the industry groups, but before moving on, it's important to understand what the Financials sector looks like globally, how it fits into a broader benchmark and how its industries fit into a broader Financials benchmark.

Global Financials Benchmarks

First, what's a benchmark? What does it do, and why is it necessary? Simply, a benchmark is your guide for building a stock portfolio.

It's a point of reference—a standard for measurement and evaluation and the investor's road map for building a stock portfolio. You can use any well-constructed index—like the MSCI World or S&P 500, for example—as a benchmark. This is just as true for a sector as it is for the broader stock market. And by studying the index's composition, you can assign expected risk and return to make underweight and overweight decisions for each category. (We'll talk more about benchmarks in Chapter 6.)

So what does the Financials investment universe look like? It depends on the benchmark. Table 1.13 shows 5 float-adjusted (i.e., excluding shares held by the government) market capitalization-weighted equity indexes, with the weight of each of the 10 market sectors. The MSCI World includes only developed countries and the EAFE only developed foreign countries. The MSCI EM and the S&P 500 are specific to Emerging Markets and the US, respectively, while the Russell 2000 is a small-capitalization US index.

Table 1.13 Equities Benchmark Comparison

	MSCI World	MSCI EAFE	MSCI EM	S&P 500 Composite	Russell 2000
Consumer Discretionary	10%	10%	8%	11%	13%
Consumer Staples	11%	12%	8%	12%	4%
Energy	12%	9%	14%	12%	7%
Financials	**18%**	**21%**	**24%**	**13%**	**21%**
Health Care	11%	10%	1%	12%	12%
Industrials	11%	12%	6%	11%	15%
Information Technology	12%	5%	13%	19%	17%
Materials	7%	10%	13%	4%	4%
Telecommunication Services	4%	6%	9%	3%	1%
Utilities	4%	5%	4%	4%	3%

Source: Thomson Reuters; MSCI, Inc.,[13] as of 12/31/2011.

Besides being the largest sector in most broad indexes, the Financials sector is also the largest sector in 19 of the 45 countries in the MSCI ACWI. Table 1.14 shows the Financials weight within each country in the MSCI ACWI. Generally, the larger the weight a sector is in a country, the more important it is to the country's economy. For example, Financials' health is highly important to countries like Hong

Table 1.14   Weight of Financials in Country

MSCI AC World Index	
Hong Kong	61%
Turkey	49%
Singapore	46%
Morocco	45%
Australia	44%
Poland	43%
Austria	42%
Colombia	42%
Spain	41%
Egypt	40%
Hungary	37%
China	36%
Peru	35%
Thailand	35%
Philippines	35%
Greece	33%
Canada	32%
Malaysia	31%
Italy	31%
Indonesia	30%
India	26%
South Africa	26%
Sweden	25%
Brazil	25%
Czech Republic	24%
Netherlands	19%

Table 1.14   Weight of Financials in Country (*Continued*)

Switzerland	18%
UK	18%
Japan	18%
Chile	17%
Germany	17%
Russia	15%
Taiwan	15%
Finland	15%
France	15%
Belgium	14%
Norway	14%
Korea	14%
US	14%
Israel	14%
Denmark	11%
Portugal	8%
Mexico	7%
Ireland	0%

Source: Thomson Reuters; MSCI, Inc.,[15] as of 12/31/2011.

Kong, Turkey, Singapore and Morocco, where the sector accounts for 45% or more of their market capitalizations.[14]

Fixed Income Benchmarks

The Financials sector accounts for substantially more assets than any other sector in the world, but it also accounts for more liabilities than any other sector. In 2011, the MSCI ACWI Financials sector had $95 trillion in liabilities. This is over four times the amount of all the other sectors' liabilities combined.[16] A large component of these liabilities is publicly traded debt instruments—bonds.

The global bond market's estimated value in 2011 was $98.7 trillion ($34 trillion domestic, $65 trillion foreign).[17] This market's scope and scale make it challenging to completely dissect, but the Bank of America Merrill Lynch Global Broad Market Index does a pretty good job (see Table 1.15). This index attempts to mimic the performance of

Table 1.15   Bank of America Merrill Lynch Global Broad Market Index Weights

Sector	Weight
Sovereign	**54%**
Securitized/Collateralized	**17%**
Quasi & Foreign Government	**12%**
Corporate—Total	**17%**
Corporate—Financials	**7%**
Banking	6%
Financial Services	1%
Insurance	1%
Corporate—Industrials	**8%**
Automotive	0%
Basic Industry	1%
Capital Goods	1%
Consumer Cyclical	1%
Consumer Non-Cyclical	1%
Energy	2%
Health Care	1%
Media	0%
Real Estate	0%
Services	1%
Technology & Electronics	0%
Telecommunications	1%
Corporate—Utility	**2%**

Source: Bank of America Merrill Lynch, as of 12/31/2011.

publicly issued investment-grade debt in major bond markets globally and is a widely used fixed income benchmark.

Unlike equity indexes, corporate bond indexes are typically grouped into three sectors rather than the 10 GICS sectors: Financials, Industrials and Utilities. When measured this way, the Financials component of the corporate bond market accounts for 44%, Industrials for 45% and Utilities for 11%.

However, when rearranged into GICS sectors, the Financials sector's dominance in the corporate bond market is clear. It accounts for

Table 1.16   Industry Group Weights Within Financial Sector Indexes

	MSCI World	MSCI EAFE	MSCI EM	S&P 500 Composite	Russell 2000
Banks	7.3%	11.3%	17.2%	2.7%	7.1%
Diversified Financials	4.0%	2.9%	2.4%	5.3%	3.1%
Insurance	3.8%	4.3%	2.6%	3.6%	3.0%
Real Estate	2.6%	3.0%	1.6%	1.9%	8.2%
Financials Sector	17.6%	21.4%	23.8%	13.4%	21.4%

Source: Thomson Reuters; MSCI, Inc.,[19] as of 12/31/2011.

41% of investment grade corporate bonds—nearly four times the size of the next-largest sector (Utilities).[18]

Being the largest sector in the bond market means nothing in itself, but it further illustrates the sector's scale. It also highlights how sensitive the sector is to trends in the bond market. Bonds are simply another way companies raise capital—the more leveraged a company is, the more impactful trends in debt markets are.

Sector Benchmarks

Sectors, just like the broader market, have their own benchmarks, and each industry constitutes a portion of the overall Financials benchmark. Also like the broader market, investors can overweight and underweight different categories based on their expected risk and return characteristics. Table 1.16 illustrates the Financials sector industry group weights in five main benchmarks.

Banks are typically the largest industry group in the Financials sector, but in the US, weights are impacted by banks that are not banks (see Chapter 2) and by the US-centric and small nature of REITs (see Chapter 5).

II

INDUSTRY GROUP DETAILS

2

BANKS

The largest industry group in most Financials sector benchmarks globally is the Bank industry group. It includes both regional and diversified banks as well as Thrifts and Mortgage Finance companies. Since they all tend to act similarly and have similar characteristics, we'll use the term *bank* to refer to firms in all of this group's sub-industries.

As Table 2.1 shows, Banks is a substantial weight in most broad equity benchmarks globally but only a small weight in the S&P 500. This is because despite having the largest domestic banks, "mega banks" like Bank of America, JP Morgan Chase & Co. and Citigroup are technically not in the Bank industry group. They're considered Diversified Financials companies, and they are very diversified—arguably no single business line is dominant. The same is true in Germany, where Deutsche Bank is also considered a Diversified Financials company. If we add these "banks" back into the industry group, the US weighting looks more like foreign benchmarks at 5.0 %.[1]

Banks, whatever their form, are the lifeblood of most economies—they facilitate the transfer and multiplication of money, payment systems, investment, leverage, etc. Beyond being a vital component of

Table 2.1   Bank Weighting Among Benchmarks

	ACWI	WORLD	EAFE	EM	S&P 500	R2K
Banks	**8.9%**	**7.31%**	**11.3%**	**17.2%**	**2.7%**	**7.1%**
Commercial Banks	8.75%	7.25%	11.3%	16.8%	2.7%	5.9%
Diversified Banks	*8.13%*	*6.55%*	*10.6%*	*16.7%*	*1.8%*	*0.0%*
Regional Banks	*0.62%*	*0.7%*	*0.6%*	*0.1%*	*0.9%*	*5.9%*
Thrifts & Mortgage Finance	0.1%	0.1%	0.0%	0.5%	0.1%	1.3%

Source: Thomson Reuters; MSCI, Inc.,[2] S&P 500, and Russell 2000 Indexes. As of 12/31/2011.

most economies and one of the largest industry groups, banks have several unique characteristics investors should be aware of, from the often confusing nature of balance sheets to robust regulatory requirements. In this chapter, we will discuss:

- Banks 101: What banks are, how they make money and types of banks
- Bank industry group characteristics
- Bank products and services
- Bank regulation

So this book is not as long as Tolkien's *Lord of the Rings* trilogy, the focus will be on the basics—by the end, you should know enough to understand how the sector works, but not enough to be a bank examiner or an insurance actuary. The focus of this chapter is on US banks, while also making note of significant differences in foreign markets when appropriate. In general, banks operate similarly across borders, though regulation can vary. Understanding US banking environment basics should provide ample knowledge that can be utilized across borders.

BANKS 101

In this section, we cover the very basics behind banking businesses. What exactly is a bank, and what differentiates it from other financial services firms? How do banks make money, and what different types of banks are there?

What Is a Bank?

Simply, a bank borrows short-term money (deposits) and makes longer-term investments (loans and securities). In doing so, banks transfer money from savers to investors (or spenders). A bank traditionally earns its income from the spread between the cost of funds (deposits) and the return on assets (loans and securities).

Loans Are Assets and Deposits Are Liabilities?

When you make a deposit into a bank account, you are lending your money to the bank. The money is still your asset, but it becomes a liability to the bank since the bank must eventually give it back to you. Conversely, when you borrow from the bank, the loan becomes your liability but is an asset to the bank.

Banks are simply big balance sheets. Therefore, managing the balance sheet is of the utmost importance. Aligning liabilities with assets and capital buffers with growth, taking appropriate credit, interest rate and currency risk—these are all things banks need to manage on a daily basis.

In the US (and most other major countries), the banking system is a *fractional reserve banking system*. This means banks take in deposits but retain only a fraction of them as a reserve. The amount banks must retain—i.e., have set aside to cover their deposits—is called the *required reserve ratio* (RRR). In the US, the ratio is 10% for retail deposits[3] (several nations' RRRs are shown in Table 2.2)—which means for every $100 in deposits, a bank must have $10 in reserve. This reserve can be in a vault or deposited at the central bank (in the US, the Federal Reserve). While the idea of an RRR is very common, there are often nuances making each calculation a bit different—for example, in the US, the RRR is calculated using "on demand" deposits, making term deposits reserve-less.

Table 2.2   Global Required Reserve Ratios

Developed Countries		Emerging Countries	
US	(0–10%)	Brazil	(4%–42%)
Israel	(0–6%)	Peru	(6%–30%)
Singapore	3.0%	China	(14%–16%)
Switzerland	2.5%	Egypt	(10%–14%)
Austria	2.0%	Colombia	(0–11%)
Belgium	2.0%	Taiwan	(4%–10.8%)
Finland	2.0%	Turkey	(5%–9%)
France	2.0%	Morocco	8.0%
Germany	2.0%	Philippines	8.0%
Greece	2.0%	Indonesia	(1%–7.5%)
Ireland	2.0%	Korea	(0–7%)
Italy	2.0%	Chile	6.6%
Netherlands	2.0%	Thailand	(0.2%–6%)
Portugal	2.0%	India	5.8%
Spain	2.0%	Poland	(0–3%)
Japan	(0.05%–1.3%)	South Africa	2.5%
Australia	0.0%	Russia	2.5%
Canada	0.0%	Hungary	2.0%
Denmark	0.0%	Czech Republic	2.0%
Hong Kong	0.0%	Malaysia	1.0%
New Zealand	0.0%	Mexico	0.0%
Norway	0.0%		
Sweden	0.0%		
UK	0.0%		

Note: Ranges are sorted by the top of the range.

Sources: International Monetary Fund, "Central Bank Balances and Reserve Requirements" (February 2011) (accessed 03/27/2012). EMU and Taiwan data from respective central banks, as of May 2011.

The rest the bank can use to make investments—e.g., making a loan or purchasing a security. This allows deposited money to be *multiplied* in an economy.

Money Multiplication   Money multiplication is essential to a healthy, growing economy. But what does that mean? Part of the 90% banks may invest (e.g., through loans or purchasing securities) may eventually make it back to a bank in the form of deposits. Then, the bank again retains 10% and re-invests the money. This can happen over and over until the limit set by the reserve requirement.

Figure 2.1 shows different reserve requirements' hypothetical impact on an initial $100 deposit. Using a 10% RRR, a bank can multiply money significantly—to nearly 10×, but just as Achilles never catches the tortoise, a 10% RRR mathematically never allows a 10× multiple. Following the same $100 through just three deposit cycles shows banks can turn $100 into nearly $350. The higher the RRR, the lower the multiplier. Some central banks actively use the RRR as monetary policy, hiking the requirement to tighten, and vice versa. This can allow for a form of regulatory arbitrage, so it is important to understand central bank policies when investing in banks.

Multiplication only happens if banks are active in their lending or investing activities. If a bank takes the $100 deposit and puts the entire amount in a vault, the $100 is essentially taken out of the system— it doesn't get lent out and re-deposited. This is what happened in the wake of the 2008 financial panic—bank reserves swelled, but lending

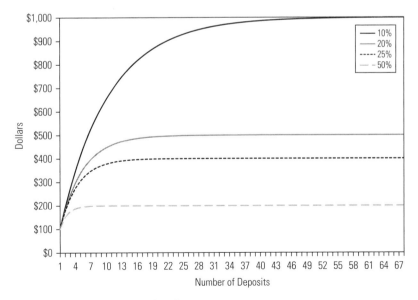

Figure 2.1   Money Multiplier

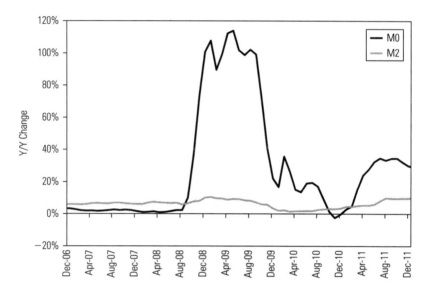

Figure 2.2   Money Supply
Source: US Federal Reserve, as of 12/31/2011.

activity remained muted, so money wasn't moving through the economy. Figure 2.2 shows even while bank reserves (as illustrated by M0) surged, the lack of multiplication suppressed broader money supply growth (as illustrated by M2).

How Do Banks Make Money?

Banks earn revenue from two main sources: *net interest income* and *non-interest income*.

Net Interest Income (NII)   Net interest income is the total of interest earned on *earning assets*—like a loan or investment securities—minus the interest costs associated with funding these assets. A common metric used in banking is the *net interest margin* (NIM), which is the interest earned on earning assets minus the interest paid on sources of funding, measured as a percentage of earning assets. For example, a bank with earning assets of $1,000 yielding $50 with funding costs at $20 would have a net interest of $30—or a NIM of 3%.

Yield Curve

A yield curve is the graphical representation of interest rates for different maturities of bonds with the same credit quality. If short-term rates are much lower than long-term, the yield curve is steep. If they are closer, the yield curve is shallow. If short-term rates are higher than long-term, the yield curve is inverted. An inverted yield curve usually means banks have less incentive to lend, and this can be a headwind to the broader economy.

A bank's NIM is driven by many factors, including the level of interest rates, the *yield curve* and the supply and demand for credit. Both sides of NIM—interest income and expense—are highly correlated to the level of intermediate-term US Treasury yields and to that of the effective US federal funds rate. The federal funds rate can be used as a proxy for a bank's cost of funds, while the Treasury yield can be used as a proxy for yield on earning assets. So shifts in the yield curve spread can drive bank NIM—up and down.

Shifts in supply and demand also impact banks' NIM. As borrowers demand more lending, banks can support higher margins. Conversely, if supply of funds outstrips demand, margins get pinched. (The Fed tracks supply and demand for credit via its quarterly Senior Loan Officer Opinion Survey [SLOOS]—available on its website.)

The mix of earning assets is also an important driver of NIM. For example, a shift from traditional residential mortgage lending into more aggressive construction/development lending can improve yield in the loan portfolio. A shift in the securities portfolio from US Treasury securities to municipal bonds can do the same. However, banks must be careful they don't increase their risk profile too much as it could drive up funding costs (and narrow the NIM) if investors start worrying about banks' risky exposures. Likewise, a shift in funding sources can impact NIM. If a bank can attract more non-interest deposits, margins could improve as funding costs move down.

In the US, net interest income averaged 65% of revenue from 1984 to 2011. However, until the 2008 financial crisis, the industry

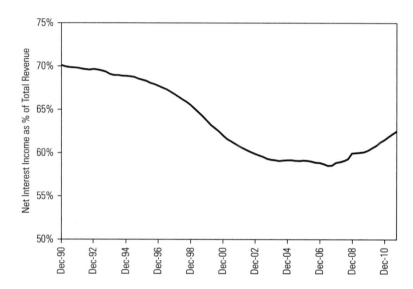

Figure 2.3   Net Interest Income as a % of Revenue

Source: Federal Deposit Insurance Corporation, "Quarterly Income and Expense of FDIC-Insured Commercial Banks and Savings Institutions," as of 12/31/2011.

increasingly focused on increasing fee income, which moved this ratio from over 70% in the 1980s to less than 60% in the 2000s (see Figure 2.3). Following the crisis, banks reverted to focusing on traditional banking (of their own accord and due to regulatory interference), thus making net interest income a growing component of revenue. While most banks earn more from interest than non-interest sources, the degree of exposures can help in determining a bank's relative interest rate sensitivity. Banks with less exposure to interest income sources can be less sensitive to interest fluctuations.

Non-Interest Income *Non-interest* income is income from non-interest bearing sources. The largest sources include services charges on deposit accounts, trading account gains and fees, fiduciary activities and net servicing fees. Other sources include revenue from non-banking sources such as investment banking, brokerage, insurance commissions or even venture capital revenue. Many of these revenue sources, like insurance and investment banking, are further explained in subsequent chapters.

Cross-Selling

Since banks offer numerous products and services, *cross-selling* and *up-selling* are core strategies used by banks. Selling an insurance product or other financial services to a client who is currently using only the bank's deposit services can greatly improve revenue and profitability. Additionally, in low interest rate environments, banks can have NIMs pinched, but selling other non-interest income products and services can greatly counter a narrowing NIM.

The Efficiency Ratio Beyond revenue sources, banks are very focused on the *efficiency ratio*—i.e., non-interest expense to revenue. It measures how much cost is associated with every unit of operating revenue. The lower the ratio, the more efficient the bank.

Large banks tend to believe banking services are commoditized, so they focus on expenses and try to maintain a low efficiency ratio. Smaller banks usually attempt to enhance the customer experience, which comes at a cost, and typically have higher efficiency ratios. In 2010, US banks on average had an efficiency ratio of 61%—big banks reported 59% and small banks reported 72%.[4]

A common M&A strategy is matching up a highly efficient bank, which supports a low efficiency ratio, with a bank with a relatively high efficiency ratio. The intended result would be synergies from implementing cost-saving initiatives in the acquired bank.

Credit Quality Credit quality, or asset quality, typically refers to the payment trends (or the expected payment trends) on a loan portfolio. The more loans going sour (or even the more loans expected to go sour), the lower the credit quality.

There are many ways to gauge credit quality: a portfolio's average FICO score, the average loan to value, average debt to income on the loans or even the structure of a portfolio (Alt-A versus 30-year fixed mortgage). To a bank, the credit quality dictates how the portfolio is likely to react to certain economic environments—which helps determine the likely portfolio yield. If you have a pool of high-yielding, low credit score credit card loans, you would anticipate greater losses in an adverse economic scenario. The trade-off is higher yield now in exchange for the risk of higher potential credit losses later.

Risk Versus Reward

In today's complex world, there is rarely a free lunch. If an asset is yielding a higher return, there is likely a corresponding increase in risk along with it. It is an efficient market we live in, and while arbitrage is possible at times, the opportunity is typically short-lived.

Same goes for Banks investors. When selecting a bank stock, one way to gauge a bank's relative riskiness is by looking at its loan portfolio's risk profile. Are they construction loans, commercial and industrial loans, mortgages or credit cards? It can make a difference, which Figure 2.4 shows. Note how the past-due rate on commercial and

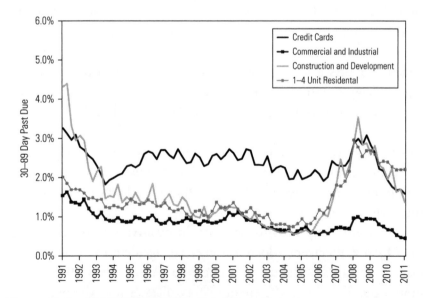

Figure 2.4   FDIC 30–89 Day Past Due Rate

Source: Federal Deposit Insurance Corporation, "Quarterly Loan Portfolio Performance Indicators, All FDIC-Insured Institutions," from 12/31/1991 to 12/31/2011.

industrial loans is much less volatile than it is on construction and development loans.

If you decide the bank has a strong loan portfolio, it could also mean it is a strong bank (of course, other things like capital and liquidity should also be considered). Sometimes this is good, sometimes bad. A strong bank doesn't always outperform a weak bank (i.e., low credit quality loans), or vice versa, but in certain market environments, one likely has the advantage. If credit quality is broadly deteriorating, the strong bank likely has the tailwind. However, if the environment is improving, the "weak bank" could witness greater return for taking the additional risk.

Monitoring key credit metrics such as the NPL ratio, NPA ratio, NPL coverage ratio (definitions to follow) and allowance-to-loans ratio is critical to understanding a bank's credit quality. When monitoring these credit metrics, it is best to pay attention to the bank's underlying quality while also comparing it to peers.

Here are a few commonly used metrics:

- The **NPL ratio** (non-performing loans/total loans) portrays loan portfolio quality—typically includes loans 30–90 days delinquent.
- The **NPA ratio** (non-performing assets/total assets) portrays asset quality, including loans and other securities.
- The **NPL coverage ratio** (loan loss reserve/non-performing loans) reveals how much a bank has set aside to cover non-performing loans if it charges them.
- When a loan moves to **nonaccrual status**, it has typically been delinquent for some time. At that point, interest is not accrued on the loan, and a realized loss is likely inevitable.
- A **net charge-off** represents the realized loss a bank takes on a loan. This number is net of "reversals," which occur when previously sour loans become good.
- The **allowance ratio** (loan loss reserve/total loans) gives insight into how much capital is set aside to cover losses stemming from a bank's total loan portfolio.

- A commonly used measurement of strength is the **Texas ratio** (non-performing assets/core equity). This scales a bank's non-performing loans to its available capital. If a bank has more non-performing loans than it does capital, this could be cause for concern.

Asset or Liability Sensitivity When a bank is "asset sensitive," its assets are more sensitive to interest rate fluctuations than its liabilities, as opposed to being "liability sensitive." If prevailing interest rates rise, an asset-sensitive bank would see its assets "re-price" quicker than its liabilities, and it would thus benefit from the move in interest rates. A bank with adjustable-rate loans funded by long-term fixed-rate bonds would be a simplistic example of an asset-sensitive bank— the interest income on the loans would increase before the interest cost of the long-term bonds does, which would allow for a widening margin. A bank funding a 10-year fixed-rate mortgage with short-term deposits would be an example of a liability-sensitive bank.

Most banks attempt to match asset and liability sensitivities (adjustable versus fixed, short versus long) so the net impact is not extreme in either direction, but even a small bet in either direction often gives a bank an edge over competition. A bank with the correct sensitivity will have a tailwind relative to peers—so be sure to consider your interest rate forecast and a bank's interest rate sensitivity when selecting a bank to invest in.

Financial Services Have Been Commoditized

In the developed world and a few developing countries, banking has become largely commoditized—meaning what you can get at one bank, you can essentially get at another, likely at a very similar price. This makes pricing powers much lower now versus a few decades ago. As a result, banks have been known to attempt personalizing the banking experience or offering businesses incentives—while receiving a free toaster for opening a checking account hasn't been common for some time, various incentives for starting or expanding a relationship with a bank are.

TYPES OF BANKS

There are many types of banks globally—construction banks, regional banks, money center banks, diversified banks, thrifts, savings and loans (S&Ls), development banks, central banks, Islamic banks … on and on. GICS segments the industry group into Commercial Banks and Thrifts & Mortgage Finance companies, but considering the very small presence of Thrifts & Mortgage Finance companies and for simplicity's sake, we'll focus on Commercial Banks, which can be further categorized as Regional and Diversified Banks.

Regional and diversified banks are very similar—size and geographic presence aside. Diversified banks are commercial banks (as opposed to investment banks) whose businesses are derived primarily from commercial lending operations and have significant business activity in retail banking and small and medium corporate lending. Regional banks are effectively the same, though typically smaller and operating in a limited geographic region, like a single city or county. Outside the US, regional banks may focus on an individual country or a specific jurisdiction within the country. For example, in Japan, the big city banks (which are considered Diversified Banks) focus on the major metro areas in Japan, as well as perhaps some overseas exposure, while many regional banks in Japan typically focus on one prefecture and surrounding areas.

Regional banks can be very small, or they can be quite large. In the US (as of this writing), the smallest reporting publicly traded regional bank had total assets of $1.7 million, while the largest had assets of $271 billion.[5] As banks increase in assets, they may be referred to as "super-regional banks," which, while not recognized by GICS, can be defined as multistate regional banks with assets large enough to be ranked as one of the 100 largest banks in the US.

Beyond becoming a super-regional bank, as banks grow in size and breadth, they can be considered *money center banks*. These banks are larger banks typically located in major financial hubs, and they offer banking services to private and public markets, including other financial institutions nationally, as well as in foreign markets.

Table 2.3 lists the world's largest banks, measured by assets. Note the absence of US banks. Table 2.4 lists the largest US banks—Wells Fargo ranks seventeenth globally based on total assets. (Remember, JP Morgan Chase & Co., Bank of America and Citigroup are not classified as *banks*. If they were, they would be ranked first, second and third domestically and eighth, tenth and twelfth globally, respectively.[6])

Table 2.3   World's Largest Publicly Traded Banks

Name	Country	Total Assets (Trillions, USD)
Mitsubishi UFJ Financial	Japan	$2.80
HSBC Holdings	UK	$2.70
BNP Paribas	France	$2.60
Royal Bank of Scotland	UK	$2.50
Barclays	UK	$2.40
Credit Agricole	France	$2.30
Industrial and Commercial Bank of China	China	$2.30
Mizuho Financial	Japan	$2.10
China Construction Bank	China	$1.80
Agricultural Bank	China	$1.80

Source: Bloomberg Finance L.P., as of 12/31/2011.

Table 2.4   America's Largest Publicly Traded Banks

Name	Total Assets (Trillions, USD)
Wells Fargo & Co.	$1.30
US Bancorp	$0.34
PNC Financial Services Group	$0.27
Suntrust Banks	$0.18
BB&T	$0.17
Regionals Financial	$0.13
Fifth Third Bancorp	$0.12
Keycorp	$0.09
M&T Bank	$0.08
Comerica	$0.06

Source: Bloomberg Finance L.P., as of 12/31/2011.

Table 2.5 briefly describes various categories of banks—which should be considered when deciding where to invest. For example, if you think the commercial & industrial (C&I) lending environment is going to be stronger than expected (due to stronger demand and better credit trends, perhaps), then it may behoove you to consider a regional bank over a savings bank or thrift due to its focus on C&I lending.

Table 2.5   Types of Banks

Types of Banks	Short Description
Commercial Bank	Focused on accepting deposits and making loans.
Regional Bank	Focused on commercial lending operations with significant business activity in retail banking, operating in a limited geographic region.
Diversified Bank	Focused on commercial lending operations with significant business activity in retail banking.
Thrift & Mortgage Finance	A broader category for Savings & Loan associations, savings banks and credit unions.
Savings & Loan	Typically similar to a commercial bank, with focus on mortgages and consumer deposits.
Savings Bank	Typically similar to a commercial bank, with focus on mortgages and consumer deposits.
Credit Union	Not-for-profit financial cooperative focused on consumer banking.
Construction Bank	A bank focusing on commercial and industrial loans, with an emphasis on construction and/or commercial real estate lending.
Money Center Bank	Larger banks located in major financial hubs offering diversified banking services to private and public markets, including other financial institutions in domestic and foreign markets.
Super-Regional Bank	Multistate regional banks with assets large enough to be ranked as one of the 100 largest banks in the US.
Islamic Bank	Banks focused on Islamic law.
Development Bank	Banks focused on financing development needs.
Investment Bank	Found in the Diversified Financials industry group (see Chapter 3).
Offshore Bank	Banks typically located in jurisdictions with low taxes and regulation.
Online Bank	A bank without physical branches, doing business online.
Business Bank	See *commercial bank*.
Postal Savings	A savings bank typically under the umbrella of a postal system. Typically functions as a bank for those without access to banks.

(Continued)

Table 2.5   Types of Banks (*Continued*)

Types of Banks	Short Description
Building Societies	Mutual institutions prevalent in the UK and other foreign markets. Focus on short-term savings and mortgages.
Merchant Bank 1	A credit card processing bank.
Merchant Bank 2	Banks involved in arranging financing but not maintaining the loans, investing in leveraged buyouts, corporate acquisitions or other structured finance. Similar to an investment bank in many regards.
Universal Bank	Sometimes called Diversified Financials companies—banks with multiple bank and non-bank business lines.

BANKS INDUSTRY GROUP CHARACTERISTICS

The Banks industry group tends to be event-driven—relative performance is a function of economic, political and sentiment events, rather than consistently outperforming or underperforming during specific market cycles. In recent decades, the S&L crisis, Asian Contagion, Tech crash, real estate boom and credit panic can explain much of the group's relative performance. In other words, this group can outperform (or underperform) during bull markets or bears, recessions or expansions—making it a difficult group to predict.

There are, however, certain characteristics that hold true over time: Size wise, it is market-like, it tends to be more value than growth, returns are often volatile and it is economically sensitive.

Size: Banks Is Market-Like

Banks, like the broader Financials sector, is market-like in size (i.e., market capitalization), if not a tad big at first glance. However, there is no discernible pattern of relative outperformance or underperformance during periods of big cap or small cap dominance. Currently, Banks' average size in the MSCI World index is $20 billion, a bit higher than the $16 billion of the broader index.[7] The median size is just a bit higher than the broader index at $8.4 billion—meaning roughly half of the banks in the index are bigger and half are smaller than the median of the broad index.[8] Conversely, the weighted average market capitalization of the MSCI World tells us a different story—measured this way, Banks is considerably smaller than the market.[9]

The big-but-small nature of the industry group is one reason Banks does not tend to follow big versus small market cycles.

Style: Banks Are Value

Banks tend to trade at low valuations, tend not to be seen as "big growth" and often pay sizable dividends—so Banks tends to perform better when value stocks overall outperform broader market indexes.

Book Value

Price to book is a very common metric used when valuing a bank as it is more stable than earnings- or revenue-based metrics. It compares a company's book value (or "net worth") to its market capitalization. A bank with a net worth of $10 billion and a market capitalization of $15 billion has a price to book of 1.5.

Price-to-book ratios vary over time, and at the time of this writing, Emerging Markets banks trade at a premium to developed world banks—mostly due to higher growth rates and profitability (see Figure 2.5).

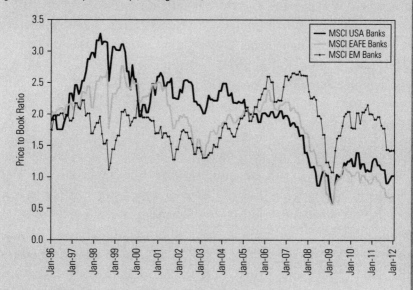

Figure 2.5   Price to Book Comparison
Source: Thomson Reuters; MSCI, Inc.,[10] as of 01/31/2012.

Furthermore, Banks historically has a higher dividend yield than most other industry groups across all sectors. Banks investors often covet dividends and use bank stocks to generate consistent cash flow over time. (Investors should remember dividends can and do get cut. In fact, many banks cut dividends in 2008 and 2009 during the credit crisis and its aftermath—and, at the time of this writing nearly four years later, banks still haven't restored dividend payouts. Remember: A dividend is not guaranteed cash flow.) From 2004 to 2011, and despite government interference, US Banks' average dividend yield of 3.0% put it in the top five dividend-paying industry groups and was much higher than the S&P 500 index's average dividend yield of 2.0%.[11] In the five years prior to the credit crisis (2004–2008), the banking industry had the second highest dividend yield, nearly twice that of the average industry.[12]

Why do banks tend to pay higher dividends? Since banks try to maintain the lowest possible cost of capital over time, paying a dividend can help attract longer-term investors—those focused on cash flow rather than growth prospects. A stable, long-term investor pool can allow banks to better forecast and control weighted-average cost of capital (WACC) and therefore maintain more consistent margins. Additionally, considering many developed-world banking environments are traditionally lower growth, dividends are a way for banks to shed excess capital and improve return on equity (ROE) by reducing the denominator side of the equation at regular intervals.

Banks Can Be Volatile

Since Banks is, by its very nature, more leveraged than any other industry group, it can be more volatile (see Table 2.6). A slight change in asset pricing (like the value of a mortgage-backed security) can have tremendous impact on a bank's capital positioning and profitability. A recent example was the horrendous impact of mark-to-market accounting rule FAS 157 (fair-value accounting) during the 2008 credit panic. Banks were forced to mark down assets based on pricing found in illiquid markets. Prices for certain assets were artificially depressed, which devastated bank balance sheets. Shares responded accordingly and plummeted during the downturn, just to spring higher after FAS 157 was watered down in March 2009.

Banks' leveraged nature, their sensitivity to regulatory whims and reliance on other people's money are why the Banks industry group is more volatile (as measured by standard deviation) than 18 of 24 standard industry groups.

Table 2.6   MSCI World Industry Group Volatility: Standard Deviation (Rolling Years, 1994–2011)

Industry	Standard Deviation
Semiconductor & Semiconductor Equipment	42%
Technology Hardware & Equipment	38%
Software & Services	33%
Diversified Financials	**28%**
Telecommunication Services	27%
Materials	26%
Real Estate	**26%**
Media	26%
Banks	**25%**
Insurance	**24%**
Capital Goods	24%
Consumer Durables & Apparel	24%
Retailing	24%
Automobiles & Components	22%
Consumer Services	22%
Energy	20%
Healthcare Equipment & Services	19%
Utilities	18%
Transportation	18%
Commercial Services & Supplies	17%
Food & Staples Retailing	17%
Food Beverage & Tobacco	16%
Pharmaceuticals, Biotechnology & Life Sciences	15%

Source: Thomson Reuters; MSCI, Inc.,[13] as of 12/31/2011.

But just like most things, the industry's volatility ebbs and flows. Much of the volatility since 1994 can be attributed to a few periods of heightened volatility: the aftermath of the Asian Contagion and the 2008–2009 financial crisis.

Banks Are Sensitive to Certain Economic Conditions

Banks are sensitive to economic conditions, but a few items stand out: interest rates, residential real estate and employment trends. Each of these can impact a bank, whether by changing supply and demand dynamics or impacting credit quality. In general, stable interest rates, a positively sloped yield curve, stable or rising home prices, increasing housing turnover and falling unemployment would provide banks substantial tailwinds.

Interest rate trends impact the cost of funds and yield on earning assets—which ultimately drive banks' margins. They also impact credit demand—a low interest rate environment encourages borrowing. As important as the shape and location of the yield curve, interest rate volatility is a headwind as widely swinging interest rates make it more difficult to manage a bank's balance sheet and maintain appropriate exposures.

Residential loans account for 33% of US bank loan portfolios, or 18% of total bank assets, making this category the largest single asset in the banking system (Federal Reserve Flow of Funds, Q4 2011 12/31/2011). Therefore, residential real estate market trends can greatly impact a bank's profitability—and, by extension, whether investors are inclined to pay a higher or lower price for the bank's stock. Periods of stable or rising home prices mean mortgages are likely to continue performing—this is a positive, or at least neutral, factor for banks. Periods when foreclosures are markedly higher mean banks risk greater losses in their mortgage portfolios, which can be a decided negative.

Moreover, the residential lending market accounts for a similarly large portion of bank income. The more loans a bank can underwrite, the better—spreads, fees and points all play a part, and this source of income is tied to loan volume.

Employment trends are also very important to most banks—they drive consumer spending, saving, delinquencies and borrowing.

A high unemployment rate can bring higher credit costs for banks. It will also pressure spending and thus can reduce borrowing— all negatively impacting banks. As the unemployment rate falls, credit losses typically fall, spending improves and lending picks up. Remember, the absolute unemployment rate is not that important— focus rather on the trend relative to expectations.

BANK REGULATION

Core drivers for all sectors, industries and companies are the same— everything can be categorized as either an economic, sentiment or political driver. How impactful each is naturally differs. The banking industry happens to be heavily influenced by political interference— primarily in the form of regulation. While the US industry is not controlled to the extent of regulated utilities, for example, recent regulatory reform is moving it in this direction. And in some countries (like China) that distinction between industries is smaller.

In the developed world, core bank regulators tend to be central banks or financial services authorities—government authorities that implement and enforce rules typically set by politicians. This makes the industry highly sensitive to political noise. Most bank regulation can be categorized as capital controls, liquidity requirements, consumer protection or structural requirements.

Given the impact politics and regulations have on banks, it's important to stay on top of current legislation as much as possible—a challenge, given its fluidity. However, a fundamental understanding is critical, so we'll touch on a few core concepts.

The Basel Committee

Ten central bank governors established the Basel Committee in 1974 in an effort to harmonize global bank regulation. Though it lacks formal supervisory authority or legal force behind its recommendations, in 1992, the committee established the Basel Capital Accord, which outlined a credit risk measurement framework and 8% minimum capital standard—it was subsequently adopted by both members and non-members. In 1999, the committee proposed changes to the framework, which came to be known as Basel II and provided a foundation for national rule making.

Basel II was based on a three-pillar framework of minimum capital requirements, a supervisory review process and market discipline. In the 2008 financial panic's wake, the Basel Committee again made changes, resulting in Basel III—which focuses on capital definitions, capital conservation buffers, countercyclical buffers, leverage ratios and global liquidity standards, among others.

A high-level understanding of the Basel Accords is critical to any bank investor, and while a full explanation is beyond this book's scope, we attempt to outline some of Basel III's major aspects here. (For more detail, refer to BIS.org.)

Definition of Regulatory Capital   Bank regulatory capital can be broken into a few core components: Common Equity Tier 1, Tier 1 and Tier 2 capital. Simply, Common Equity Tier 1 and additional Tier 1 are *going concern capital*, while Tier 2 capital consists of more debt-like capital and is considered *gone concern capital*. Whereas going concern capital can absorb losses while the bank is a going concern, gone concern capital absorbs losses only after a bank fails. Consider the difference between holding equity (shares) and debt (bonds): Banks' losses would detract from shareholders' equity, but bondholders would eventually get their money back unless there was a default.

As of this writing, Basel III set minimum capitalization ratios (the ratio between the equity level and risk-weighted assets) for Common Equity Tier 1, Tier 1 and total capital at 4.5%, 6.0% and 8.0%, respectively.

Risk-Adjusted Balance Sheets   Many regulatory capital ratios, such as the Tier 1 capital ratio, rely on risk-adjusted assets rather than total assets. In the US, this means many regulatory capital ratios are based on $9.4 trillion (risk adjusted) rather than $13.8 trillion (total assets).[14] The premise behind risk adjusting a balance sheet is some assets are simply riskier than others—some have a much higher probability of default (POD) and/or higher expected recovery values. Consider the difference in credit risk between a US Treasury security, a pool of residential mortgages and a pool of credit card loans. The Treasury has the full faith and credit of the United States of America, which is the safest of the three. Mortgages tend to be higher quality than credit cards not just because the borrower often has a vested interest in paying the mortgage, but also because of the collateral—the underlying real estate has value, and if the mortgage defaults, the lender is only on the hook for the difference between the mortgage loan and the property value. The credit card is not "collateralized" and therefore is the riskiest of the three.

As a result, the Treasury will have the smallest risk weighting, followed by the mortgage then the credit card. And since each of these exposures has significantly different risk, the capital required for each is different—the same capital *ratio* is required for each, but it is based on the risk-adjusted value of the exposure. (See Appendix C for more detail on risk weightings.)

Capital Conservation Buffer   Basel III introduced a capital conservation buffer of 2.5% over and above minimum capital requirements, bringing the required Common Equity Tier 1, Tier 1 and total capital ratios to 7.0%, 8.5% and 10.5%, respectively. The buffer's intent is to protect depositors as opposed to shareholders in the event a bank lends beyond minimum capital requirements. As a bank's capital ratio falls below its required buffer, it must increasingly restrict distributions, which determines how much of earnings the bank must conserve the following year.

Countercyclical Buffer   Basel III also introduced a countercyclical buffer that aims to ensure capital requirements account for macrofinancial economic conditions. In other words, this buffer adds up to an additional 2.5% to minimum capital ratios in the event countries believe aggregate credit growth is excessive.

Leverage Ratio   As opposed to other capital ratios that use a risk-adjusted balance sheet, the leverage ratio (which is being tested at 4% from 2013 to 2017) compares Tier 1 capital to *total* assets and would limit outright bank leverage regardless of how much risk it takes. This could negatively impact more conservative banks because near credit risk-free investments would receive the same weight as high-risk investments.

Global Liquidity Standards   The liquidity coverage ratio (LCR) is expected to be implemented by mid-2013 and is designed to prevent bank runs by ensuring banks have sufficient unencumbered, high-quality assets. So while a bank run likely conjures scenes from *It's a Wonderful Life* for most, banks today back assets with more than just deposits.

The LCR mandates the total of high-quality liquid assets must always exceed total net outflows over the next 30 days—in other words, it ensures banks always have enough cash equivalents to support total cash needs for the next 30 days.

On the other hand, the net stable funding ratio (NSFR) focuses on longer-term funding profiles in an attempt to reduce reliance on short-term funding. Considering the highly debated costs of the ratio, the NSFR has been pushed off to 2018.[15]

As it stands now, the committee wants Basel III to be implemented in stages, as illustrated in Table 2.7.

National regulators will set their own rules and determine their own timelines, though often based on the committee's recommendations. This can allow for regulatory arbitrage while certain countries' banks have a relative advantage over global peers.

Liquidity

Since banks are in the business of borrowing short and lending long, their liquidity (or their ability to meet current obligations) is more important than firms' in any other industry group.

The banking system is built upon trust: Depositors trust banks to return deposits upon demand, and banks trust other financial institutions in the same way. If this trust is broken or doubted, banks' funding sources could become much more expensive or even dry up,

Table 2.7 Basel III Implementation Timeline—Phase-in Arrangements

	2011	2012	2013	2014	2015	2016	2017	2018	As of January 1, 2019
Leverage Ratio			Parallel Run January 1, 2013–January 1, 2017 Disclosure Starts 1 Jan 2015					Migration to Pillar 1	
Minimum common equity capital ratio			3.5%	4.0%	4.5%	4.5%	4.5%	4.5%	4.5%
Capital conversion buffer						0.625%	1.25%	1.875%	2.50%
Minimum common equity plus capital conservation buffer			3.5%	4.0%	4.5%	5.125%	5.75%	6.375%	7.0%
Phase-in of deductions from CET1 (including amounts exceeding the limit for DTAs, MSRs and financials)				20%	40%	60%	80%	100%	100%
Minimum tier 1 capital			4.5%	5.5%	6.0%	6.0%	6.0%	6.0%	6.0%
Minimum total capital			8.0%	8.0%	8.0%	8.0%	8.0%	8.0%	8.0%
Minimum total capital plus conversion buffer			8.00%	8.00%	8.00%	8.625%	9.25%	9.875%	10.5%

(*Continued*)

57

Table 2.7 Basel III Implementation Timeline—Phase-in Arrangements (Continued)

	2011	2012	2013	2014	2015	2016	2017	2018	As of January 1, 2019
Leverage Ratio			Parallel Run January 1, 2013–January 1, 2017 Disclosure Starts 1 Jan 2015					Migration to Pillar 1	
Capital instruments that no longer qualify as non-core Tier 1 capital or Tier 2 capital									
Liquidity coverage ratio	Observation period begins				Introduce minimum standard				
Net stable funding ratio	Observation period begins							Introduce minimum standard	

Shading indicates transition periods. All dates are as of January 1.
Source: Bank for International Settlements, as of 12/2011.

like in 2008. Bank deposits, traditionally a core funding source, are usually insured to a degree, but other forms of funding are not—typically referred to as "wholesale funding." Wholesale funding is derived from other financial institutions—like borrowing from a bank, borrowing in the repo or commercial paper markets or even borrowing directly from a central bank or other government entity.

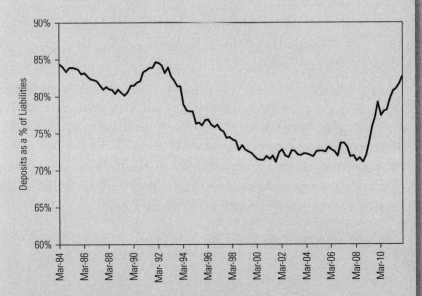

Deposit Funding

Thanks to financial innovation over the decades, banks have come to rely less on deposits as a core funding source. From 1984 to 2008, deposits went from 85% of liabilities to just 71%.[16] Following 2008's financial panic, deposits surged to 80%, reversing a nearly two decade-long trend in about a year (see Figure 2.6). Deposits' stability coupled with many wholesale funding sources' seizing up drove much of the rapid shift. Bank regulation changes and fears of future changes also contributed.

Figure 2.6   FDIC Banks' Total Deposits as a % of Total Liabilities

Source: Federal Deposit Insurance Corporation, "Quarterly Banking Profile," as of 09/31/2011.

Interbank Lending Rates

Interbank lending is the industry's lifeblood, allowing banks to manage liquidity needs daily and central banks to implement monetary policy.

Uncollateralized interbank lending is just what it sounds like: One bank lends to another on the borrowing bank's word and the loan will be repaid with interest at the scheduled maturity date. These rates are not set by any governing body, but typically a central bank's target rate will provide the foundation for overnight rates. These reference rates are expected to portray perceived borrowing rates between banks on an uncollateralized basis over multiple maturities in specific currencies and markets—this is not the rate at which banks *actually* borrow, but rather the rate at which banks *expect* they would borrow if the need arose. Interbank offered rates (IBOR) are reference rates set by a panel of banks operating in a specific market—e.g., LIBOR in London, the EURIBOR in Europe, TIBOR in Tokyo and SIBOR in Singapore—each similar but using its own methodology.

The reference rate is an annualized rate, so if the overnight EURIBOR is at 1.0%, this means an overnight loan would cost 0.0027% (1.0%/365 days). Which might sound cheap, but for a bank borrowing €25 billion for one day, it would equate to €684,931.51.

Liquidity can be measured various ways. The loan-to-deposit (LDR) ratio compares total deposits to total loans and demonstrates how much of a bank's loan portfolio is funded with deposits rather than other sources. A ratio lower than 100% indicates the bank funds its entire loan portfolio via deposits—meaning that bank would likely be less impacted by trends in wholesale funding markets. When liquidity is scarce (or expensive), a low LDR can be a significant advantage.

That CD Has a High Rate for a Reason

Banks manipulate deposit rates based on liquidity needs. Often, when a bank needs to attract more liquidity, it increases its advertised rates on deposits to make the bank more attractive to depositors. This attracts yield-chasing depositors and provides the bank with

(Continued)

the desired liquidity. Banks typically do not want to pay more than they have to for liquidity, so an above-market CD yield could imply the bank is a higher-risk bank—investors are demanding more compensation. As you could expect, yield-chasing depositors are not stable forms of funding—the bank will either need to maintain higher-than-market interest rates or risk losing the liquidity to someone else.

Other measurements are the core funding ratio or the non-interest-bearing deposits ratio. Core funding refers to funding from retail deposits—which tend to be more stable funding. Non-interest-bearing deposits (typically traditional checking accounts as well as some escrow or payroll accounts) can help margins—the more the better.

All of these ratios give insight into a bank's liquidity profile. For example, if you are looking for a bank that may not be impacted by liquidity concerns, you may focus on low-LDR banks with high core deposit ratios. Or if you think short-term interest rates are likely to rise and potentially pressure margins, banks with ample non-interest-bearing deposits would have a leg up.

3

DIVERSIFIED FINANCIALS

The Diversified Financials industry group is the "catchall" of the Financials sector. If it doesn't fit neatly in the Banking, Insurance or Real Estate groups, it's labeled a diversified. Although the group is diverse enough to capture pawn shops and nationally recognized statistical rating organizations (NRSRO), the vast majority of the group is made up of capital markets-related and multi-faith conglomerates. Using GICS classifications, the group consists of Capital Markets, Consumer Finance and Diversified Financial Services industries (see Table 3.1).

The group is very top-heavy: The largest 10 Diversified Financials firms account for nearly 60% of the industry group's weight in the MSCI ACWI. And of this, over half is attributed to the US banks that are not categorized as banks—Citigroup, Bank of America and JP Morgan Chase & Co.

This chapter covers the following sub-industries, delving into the characteristics of each:

Table 3.1   Diversified Financials Composition

	MSCI World	MSCI EAFE	MSCI EM	S&P 500 Composite	Russell 2000
Diversified Financials	3.98%	2.87%	2.37%	5.26%	3.10%
Capital Markets	1.70%	1.73%	0.58%	1.81%	1.91%
Consumer Finance	0.42%	0.04%	0.12%	0.77%	0.77%
Diversified Financial Services	1.86%	1.09%	1.67%	2.68%	0.42%

Source: Thomson Reuters; MSCI, Inc.;[1] Russell 2000 and S&P 500 Indexes. As of 12/31/2011.

- Capital Markets
  - Asset Managers & Custody Banks
  - Investment Banking & Brokers
  - Diversified Investment Banking
- Consumer Finance
- Diversified Financial Services

CAPITAL MARKETS

The Capital Markets industry is home to Asset Managers & Custody Banks, Investment Banking (IB) & Brokers and Diversified Capital Markets sub-industries. These businesses often overlap—e.g., a diversified capital markets firm could run an IB, several asset management companies, a custody bank and even a commercial bank! Breaking the business apart by unit helps determine what drivers will be more important.

All three sub-industries are impacted by trends in capital markets, meaning rising asset prices and increased capital markets activity are generally a boon. The trick is picking which one is most exposed to areas you forecast to do best. For example, if you forecast stocks will go up in the period ahead, perhaps an asset manager would be a suitable investment. If you believe M&A activity will pick up, maybe look into the investment banks. And if you think trading will be robust, you'd probably look at the brokers.

Asset Managers & Custody Banks

Asset managers' and custody banks' primary business is safekeeping and managing other people's money (OPM). Whereas the asset managers typically have a degree of control over client funds, custody banks do not and act more as custodians and order takers.

Both asset managers and custody banks can have varying degrees of exposure. Often, a commercial bank can serve as custody bank and retail bank, or an asset manager may be an asset manager first and private bank second. The degree of exposure will help determine how the company will act in various market environments.

Asset Managers   Asset managers are firms set up to manage investors' wealth in pursuit of their investment objectives. Most asset managers derive their revenue via a fee based on the amount of client assets under management (AUM).

AUM composition is a telltale sign of how the manager will act in different market conditions. For example, fixed-income managers may outperform equity managers in equity bear markets, and vice versa—though that's not uniformly true. Many managers manage a combination of equities and fixed income—the degree to which each is exposed will determine how it acts. Same goes for alternative money managers—those focused on private equity, real estate, commodities or even currencies will act differently depending on the underlying asset type's performance. While there are several classes of assets, a plethora of possibilities, most publicly traded asset managers focus on stocks, bonds or a combination of the two.

Worldwide Assets Invested in Mutual Funds

Globally, the US market makes up just under half of total mutual fund assets (see Table 3.2), which include mutual funds, exchange traded funds, closed-end funds and unit investment trusts (UITs).

(Continued)

Table 3.2   Makeup of Worldwide Mutual Fund Assets

Region	AUM (bil, US$)	Weight
Total	$24,699	
US	11,821	48%
Europe	7,903	32%
Asia and Pacific	3,067	12%
Other Americas	1,766	7%
Africa	142	1%

Source: Investment Company Institute, "2011 Investment Company Fact Book: A Review of Trends and Activity in the Investment Company Industry" (51st ed.) (accessed March 28, 2012).

When considering asset managers, one of the first things to determine is which asset class you expect will outperform. If you believe equities will outperform, it doesn't matter if you pick the best performing fixed-income manager—the stock of that firm likely faces significant headwinds. Further analysis should include trends on net flows, style and performance.

As the old adage goes, "A rising tide lifts all boats"—meaning if equities are higher, it is likely most equity-focused asset managers experience a tailwind to AUM growth. This is one reason it is important to pay attention to net flows, or the value of new sales minus redemptions plus net exchanges—a positive number represents a positive flow, and vice versa. Net flows measurement is important because it strips out the impact of market fluctuations and shows how much new business the manager captured during the period.

Not Credit Sensitive

Pure Asset Managers is unique in the sense it's one of the few Financials sub-industries not typically tied to credit quality, as opposed to banks or consumer lenders. Nor do asset managers commonly hold portfolios of securities for their own investment purposes. If you believe credit quality is going to weaken or credit spreads will widen, managers would have a relative advantage versus other areas directly impacted.

Style can refer to active versus passive, value versus growth, small versus big, foreign versus domestic or even quantitative versus traditional management styles. As with asset class selection, the manager's style could very well drive the firm's relative performance. If you expect large US growth companies to outperform, selecting an asset manager with a similar strategy will give you a leg up if your outlook is correct.

Investors tend to prefer to invest in firms that have done well over time. If an asset manager has a strong performance record, it is much easier to attract new clients. An industry standard for tracking performance is to measure performance relative to similar investments. Typically, a higher rating supports net flows, and vice versa. However, all investors should be aware past performance is no guarantee of future returns, and while a strong track record could help attract client funds, focusing on a manager's strategy moving forward relative to your outlook is equally important.

Distribution is also important for an asset manager. Often managers offer their product through a third-party channel, which can help in gathering assets but pinches margins. It also puts the manager at risk if any one channel controls a significant portion of its flows. If a major brokerage firm controls 50% of a manager's flow, the manager could lose some of its autonomy.

Another thing to consider is the manager's customer base. Is the manager a mutual fund catering to retail investors, a separate account manager focused on serving institutional investors or a hedge fund serving the affluent? Understanding the end market's trends can also help in your selection.

Talent

An asset manager is only as good as its talent. A stable talent pool can be a strategic attribute. If talent is jumping ship, make sure you understand what impact it could have and, more importantly, why.

A core revenue source for asset managers is typically management fees, followed perhaps by performance fees and other miscellaneous

Table 3.3   Fund Expense Ratios for Selected Investment Objectives

Investment Objective	Average
Equity funds	1.5%
Aggressive growth	*1.5%*
Growth	*1.4%*
Sector funds	*1.7%*
Growth and income	*1.3%*
Income equity	*1.3%*
International equity	*1.6%*
Hybrid funds	*1.3%*

Source: Investment Company Institute, 2011 Investment Company Fact Book: A Review of Trends and Activity in the Investment Company Industry (51st ed.) (accessed March 28, 2012).

revenues. These fees are usually based on a percentage of AUM and vary depending on investment objective. Table 3.3 illustrates the average fee charged by the mutual fund industry in 2010.

Since most revenue is generated through a fee based on AUM, AUM is the driving force behind asset manager valuations. The amount, growth rate and characteristics of AUM will help in determining an asset manager's value. Actively managed AUM usually demands a higher multiple than passive AUM, and equity AUM has a higher value than fixed or short-term AUM. Understanding all of these will give you a leg up in investing in this sub-industry.

Balance Sheet Snapshot

Pure asset managers are not capital-intensive and do not require a lot of hard assets. The largest component of a balance sheet is usually *intangibles,* such as goodwill, the value of client relationships and advisory contracts as well as brand names, technologies and trademarks.

Custody Banks As of this writing, there are only three custody banks in the MSCI ACWI—Bank of NY Mellon, Northern Trust and State Street. All are financial holding companies consisting of commercial banking and trust subsidiaries. While the commercial banking subsidiaries will act similar to other commercial banks, the trust companies offer unique services over and above what a commercial bank can offer. These companies also own asset management subsidiaries and other financial operations.

Custodial services include safekeeping, recordkeeping, pricing, shareholder services, trade settlement, reporting, trust services, cash management, risk and performance analytical services, operations outsourcing, securities lending … the list goes on and on. Like asset managers, custody banks derive their revenue from OPM, but rather than AUM, custody banks refer to assets under custody (AUC). A big difference between AUM and AUC is custodians do not manage AUC—rather, they hold them for safekeeping and perhaps processing or reporting purposes. As a result, fees on AUC are typically much, much lower than those on AUM.

Two core drivers of custody banking are asset values and interest rates. A considerable portion of revenue is derived from a fee based on AUC—as AUC increases, so do fees. Additionally, several custodian bank services are driven by NIM, such as securities lending, and as the yield curve steepens, margins follow. Furthermore, due to custodial services, custody banks tend to be less credit sensitive than commercial banks but less impacted by trends in capital markets than asset managers or investment banks.

Assets Under Custody

Although there are only the three banks classified as custody banks in the MSCI AC index, they collectively have $52 trillion in AUC.[2]

Investment Banking & Brokerage

Investment banks and brokers are very sensitive to capital markets activity. In general, they both tend to do well as markets and corporate sentiment are improving with expectations for higher asset values, improved margins and increased activity.

Investment Banks   In their purest form, investment banking activities include underwriting securities and advisory services. However, when most investors think about an investment bank now, the names Goldman Sachs and Morgan Stanley likely come to mind. It is true these financial companies operate some of the world's largest and most successful investment banks. However, traditional investment banking is a small part of what they do. In 2011, traditional investment banking net revenue accounted for 15% and 13% of these companies' total net revenue, respectively.[3] In addition to investment banking, asset management and commercial banking, they also offer client trading, brokerage and security services, and they run proprietary trading desks and make principal investments ... this is not a sub-industry for the lighthearted.

Securities underwriting is the business of raising capital from investors on behalf of a client issuing securities. These securities are typically either equity-like or debt-like. Sometimes the investment bank managing the issue will underwrite the entire deal, and sometimes the managing bank will enlist a group of banks, or a syndicate, to fund the securities.

Underwriting securities is a lucrative business: In 2011, investment banks globally earned $16 billion in equity-related and $2 billion in debt-related underwriting gross fee income. Fees are typically calculated as a percent of dollar volume underwritten—e.g., in 2011, global equities underwriting dollar volume was $442 billion. The $16 billion in fee income corresponds to an average 3.57% fee. Debt underwriting volume was $758 billion and averaged a 0.27% fee.[4]

To an investment bank, advisory services can mean many things. The most common advisory service, in both number of deals and

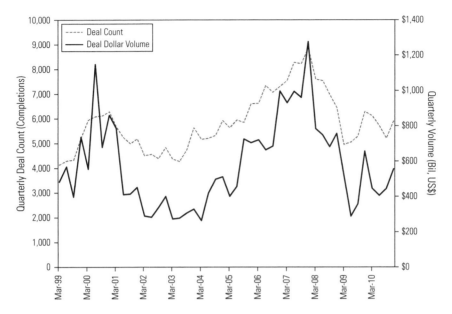

Figure 3.1   Global M&A Activity 1999–2011
Source: Bloomberg Finance L.P., as of 12/31/2011.

dollar volume, is company takeovers, which accounted for 55% of reported "deals" in 2011.[5] Other types of advisory services include advising on mergers, spin-offs and asset sales.

An increase in underwriting activity is clearly a good thing for the investment banks, as are increased M&A and other advisory activity, but keep in mind how exposed the investment bank is to this type of activity. Correctly forecasting a spike in these activities could give you a leg up when investing in Financials.

Client Execution (FICC)   FICC is a common acronym for fixed income, currencies and commodities. This business usually refers to client-driven trading operations in these markets. The investment banks act as broker, agent, market maker or even simply facilitator of client trades in these markets. Since many of these markets are found OTC (over the counter), unlike most equities, the nature of FICC can be a bit opaque at times. These markets can be defined as liquid, less liquid or custom.

Liquid markets, such as the US Treasury market, are high-volume markets, and investment banks typically charge a small fee or spread to facilitate a transaction. Less liquid markets are more difficult to navigate, so the banks make higher spreads. Custom transactions can be client-driven and usually tailor-made to address a client's specific needs—these are typically illiquid investments and not intended to have a secondary market. Investment banks can simply facilitate the transaction—they may make a market in the security, or perhaps they own an inventory, and perhaps they will take the other side of the transaction. Being able to play all sides allows the investment banks to appropriately manage their risk … and make money.

Government Action: The Volcker Rule

Many commercial banks operate investment banking operations, and conversely, many investment banks operate commercial banks. The two businesses are complementary and allow for substantial synergies. As a result of the 2008 credit panic, and as part of the Dodd-Frank Bill, the Volcker Rule was enacted, which attempts to reduce investment banking activity by banks. However, as of this writing, the rule remains undefined and unimplemented.

Principal Investments/Trading   Since investment banks can take the "other side of the trade" and maintain an inventory, they often run proprietary trading desks where they use their own money to invest, trade and otherwise turn a profit. The banks also often make long-term proprietary investments. These can be strategic in nature, such as creating a joint venture with a Chinese bank to gain Chinese influence, or simply investments similar to individual investors'.

These investing activities were brought into the lime light when the Dodd-Frank Act introduced the Volcker Rule. In its purest form, the Volcker Rule attempts to reduce or eliminate US banks' ability to take on proprietary investments. The idea behind the rule is it is unfair, and perhaps unsafe, to allow banks to benefit from FDIC insurance on deposits (which provides stable and cheap funding for the banks), just to turn around and invest in a "risky" investment. If the "risky" investment goes sour and bankrupts the bank, FDIC insurance kicks in and indemnifies depositors up to certain limits. Moreover, there is a belief if the firm were deemed too big to fail, the US government would ultimately be forced to bail it out at the expense of US taxpayers.

Definitions are the key—how does one define proprietary trades or principal investments, or how does an investment become classified as "risky"? These questions are a big part of the Volcker Rule's implementation delay and will likely create some confusion even after they are answered.

The Volcker Rule does, however, allow for market making and hedging—which often blur the line with proprietary trading. In a market-making operation, the bank facilitates trades and provides liquidity. The bank acts as the market and matches buyers with sellers—and sometimes, when there is no match, it steps in and takes the other side of the trade to allow an orderly market. When this happens, the bank takes a risk for a short time.

A proprietary trade could look very similar to market-making operations—the bank may intentionally place a trade (buy or sell) in an effort to close the trade out at a profit—but the intent is different. The Volcker Rule attempts to limit or eliminate proprietary trading—but one wonders how it can be reasonably distinguished from market-making operations and therefore reliably enforced.

Additionally, the Volcker Rule allows firms to hedge risks. However, just as we found out from JP Morgan Chase & Co in May 2012, hedges do not always work. Hedges are usually offsetting positions intended to reduce risk. But they're not always linked to the risks (or assets) being hedged—making it difficult to delineate between a hedge and a proprietary trade.

Value at Risk

Investment banks report VaR, or "value at risk," which represents the hypothetical (often a 1% or 5% probability) risk of loss over a specified period of time. As the banks ratchet up VaR, they are taking bigger bets—this can be a blessing or a curse, depending on how their bets pan out.

Brokerage

Within the Capital Markets industry, a brokerage firm is typically engaged in many components of the investment process, including securities distribution and trading, financial planning, asset management, custodial services, research and even commercial banking and insurance services. Some brokerages are stand-alone companies, but many are part of larger conglomerates—determining the degree of exposure to revenue sources is important.

There are two core types of brokerages: full service and discount. They typically offer similar services, but as the names imply, discount brokers offer less expensive choices, while full-service brokers may offer more products and services. Most often, discount brokers offer much of their product online with very little personal interaction. Full-service brokers may tout a more "personal touch."

The broader trends for both are very similar. As investors have more money to invest, brokers benefit through rising asset prices, more investors or by increased savings rates. Additionally, brokers can benefit from stealing market share from competitors.

Brokers can charge fees or spreads or collect commissions on investment products. Some brokers focus on fee-based services, which can add a degree of stability to revenue since the fee is typically a set percentage of managed money. Others are more transaction based, charging a commission on each purchase or sale, which makes revenue more volatile—but if trading volumes pick up, it could be a boon.

Free Trades!

Thanks to financial innovation, pure brokerage services have become commoditized to the point many brokers are able to offer very cheap transactions—sometimes at no cost to the investor. Understanding nothing is truly free in this world, "free" trading needs to make financial sense to a broker. Whether the broker sells stock out of inventory to make a profit on the transaction or the free trades are a lure in hopes of cross-selling, or whether there are even increased fees elsewhere, brokers would not offer free trades unless it was economically beneficial.

Since brokers typically offer myriad products and services, many economic factors can have varying impacts based on exposure—specific to the industry, daily average trades, net new client assets and the number of new accounts.

As with the Asset Management sub-industry, Brokers benefits from rising asset prices. As asset prices improve, investors have more money to invest and brokers collect more revenue accordingly. Also similar to asset management, the sub-industry is less subject to credit quality. Although some brokers will offer lending services and can at times invest in securities, most are less exposed to credit losses than a commercial bank, investment bank or consumer lending company—this makes Brokers a bit less exposed to credit losses than Banks, but typically more than Asset Managers.

Diversified Capital Markets

Diversified Capital Markets is a sub-industry encompassing firms with a significant presence in multiple capital market activities. These firms act according to their exposures and are a good way of getting broad capital markets exposure.

The vast majority of the sub-industry is composed of three firms: Credit Suisse, Deutsche Bank and UBS. These firms are large financial conglomerates offering commercial, private and investment banking, as well as asset management and other financial services.

CONSUMER FINANCE

Consumer Finance is a small part of the Financials sector, but as with other Diversified Financials firms, many larger companies take part in the business of consumer finance.

This industry is in the business of providing credit to consumers. Consumer finance includes credit cards, student lending, auto loans, home equity loans, lines of credit and personal loans. This credit can typically be divided into *revolving* and *non-revolving*.

Revolving credit refers to credit cards or lines of credit and accounts for 32% of outstanding US consumer credit.[6] With revolving credit, the borrower can borrow up to a limit or pay down the loan at any time. In fact, the debt could last indefinitely if the borrower and lender so choose. The remaining 68% of consumer debt is considered non-revolving credit—loans that can be drawn down only once and have scheduled repayment—e.g., a typical auto loan.[7]

Although Consumer Finance is an industry unto itself, in the US, the Banking industry holds most of the outstanding consumer loans, followed by finance firms and last the government (mainly through student lending). (See Figure 3.2.) Since consumer lending is offered through multiple sub-industries, understanding trends here can help investors understand the consumer loan portion of a company's overall loan portfolio.

Student Loan Marketing Association (Sallie Mae)

SLM Corporation was once known as the Student Loan Marketing Association, or Sallie Mae. It was a government-sponsored enterprise with a goal of increasing access to higher education by acting as a secondary market for student loans. In 2004, the company was privatized and ties with the government severed. Since then, the government has become a bigger holder of student debt as it now issues loans directly rather than using the secondary market created by SLM.[8]

The investable universe in this industry is rather limited: There are fewer than 100 Consumer Finance firms with a market capitalization

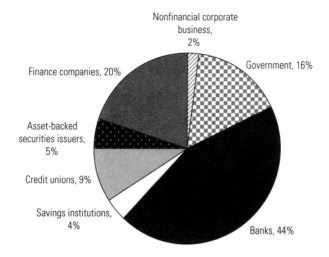

Figure 3.2   Holders of US Consumer Credit 2011

Source: US Federal Reserve, Flow of Funds Accounts of the United States: Flows and Outstandings Third Quarter 2011 (accessed 03/27/2012).

greater than $100 million globally.[9] These firms range from credit card companies to student lenders to payday loan companies to pawnshops. While the type of consumer credit offered varies, they all provide either revolving or non-revolving credit to consumers.

Aside from regulation and interest rates, both of which can impact profitability and viability, a core driver for consumer lenders is obviously consumers. Are consumers borrowing more or less? How is their ability to service debt payments? Do consumers have jobs? Consumer health is core to the industry—it drives credit loss and loan growth.

As a lending-based industry, the quality of loans is a critical component of return, and a core determinant of loan quality is employment. As consumers can't find or keep jobs, delinquency rates tend to (though not always) move higher and consumer lending companies need to provision for potential losses. And as covered in Chapter 2, provisioning reduces profitability. Accordingly, the relationship between the US employment rate and 30-day credit card delinquencies is very strong.[10] (See Figure 3.3.)

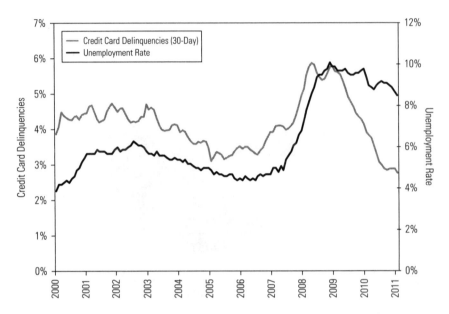

Figure 3.3   US Credit Card Delinquencies and Unemployment
Source: Bloomberg Finance L.P., US Bureau of Labor Statistics, as of 12/31/2011.

Beyond employment, consumer spending and savings trends impact the industry by shifting aggregate demand for consumer credit. When consumers spend, it's often done via credit. Furthermore, if savings rates are high, spending could be crimped and the demand for credit decline.

Consumer Finance firms are not mortgage lenders—this is a key distinguishing factor. Banks are typically heavily exposed to real estate lending, which exposes them to trends therein. If you want exposure to the lending environment but do not want exposure to real estate, the Consumer Finance industry is a pretty good way to go. However, be careful—while Consumer Finance firms do not typically offer mortgages, often the parent company or the holding company has a banking subsidiary. Make sure you understand the parent company's total exposure whenever you invest in the Financials sector.

Consumer Finance firms aren't depository institutions, meaning they do not typically accept deposits. Instead, they rely on other funding sources, like issuing bonds or asset-backed securities, to fund

Debt Service and Financial Obligation Ratios

In the US, the Federal Reserve provides debt service and financial obligations ratios (see Figure 3.4). The household debt service ratio (DSR) is an estimate of the ratio of debt payments to disposable personal income. The financial obligations ratio (FOR) adds automobile lease payments, rental payments on tenant-occupied property, homeowners' insurance and property tax payments to the debt service ratio. Both are intended to gauge a household's exposure and ability to make good on debt obligations.

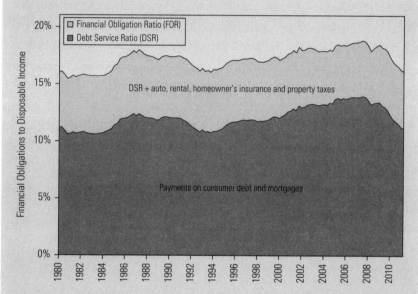

Figure 3.4   Financial Obligation and Debt Service Ratio

Source: US Federal Reserve, "Household Debt Service and Financial Obligations Ratios," as of 12/31/2011 (accessed March 28, 2012).

lending initiatives. Relative to banks, this puts them at a funding disadvantage since they don't have access to relatively cheap deposit funding. But this also means they are not under the umbrella of the bank regulators and don't have to abide by "bank" regulations—although regulation post-2009 is heading that way.

Since Consumer Finance is often "higher risk" lending—non-secured credit cards or loans secured with depreciating assets (like automobiles)—the industry typically charges higher interest rates on loans. This allows Consumer Finance firms to get away with higher net interest margins—but considering increased risk brings with it increased expected credit losses, the trade-off overall seems fair.

DIVERSIFIED FINANCIAL SERVICES

The Diversified Financial Services industry is home to the Multi-Sector Holdings, Other Diversified Financials and Specialized Finance sub-industries. Collectively, it accounts for roughly half the Diversified Financials industry group in the MSCI World Index.[11] This industry may include firms like stock exchanges, nationally recognized statistical rating organizations (NRSROs) and specialty lenders, but the vast majority of the industry is represented by the US banks that are not banks—JP Morgan Chase and Co., Bank of America and Citigroup. These three firms alone account for 1.2% of the MSCI World Index, 30% of the Diversified Financials Industry group and 88% of the Diversified Financial Services industry.[12] These three Diversified Financials firms derive their revenue and income from a diversified pool of businesses, encompassing most of the business lines in the Financials sector.

Systemically Important Financial Institutions (SIFI)

With collectively more than $6.3 trillion in assets, JP Morgan & Chase Co., Citigroup and Bank of America are among other financial behemoths deemed systemically important financial institutions (SIFI), also known as global systemically important banks (G-SIBs).[13] This title implies the failure of one of these institutions would have systemic consequences. And with their collective total assets amounting to about 50% of total US commercial banking assets, this assessment seems reasonable.[14]

There are pros and cons to being deemed SIFI. The pro is the perceived safety net (which the government is attempting to remove); the con is the recent push to increase the capital requirements of SIFI to account for the systemic risk.

If you think large cap will outperform, this sub-industry may be appropriate—it doesn't get much larger in the Financials sector—or in most others, for that matter. The average market cap of the Diversified Financial Services sub-industry is the second largest in the MSCI World Index, second to only the Energy sector's Integrated Oil and Gas sub-industry.[15]

4

INSURANCE INDUSTRY GROUP

T he Insurance Industry group includes five sub-industries. Each has unique characteristics, but all are involved in the business of transferring risk. Further, the core of the group is Life & Health Insurance (L&H) and Property & Casualty Insurance (P&C). The other three sub-industries are derivatives of these two: the Brokers sub-industry sells the insurance, Reinsurance offers insurance to insurers and Multiline Insurers is a combination of insurers.

Definition: Indemnification

Indemnification is the act of compensating for actual loss or damage.

Accordingly, in most major global indexes, the largest sub-industries are typically L&H and P&C, combined averaging about 70% of the Insurance weight.[1] Additionally, because most insurance industries are similar across the globe and the US is the world's largest insurance market (about 35% of the global market),[2] much of this chapter will focus on the US.

This chapter covers the characteristics of the two major sub-industries but also touches on the smaller groups. Topics include:

- Characteristics of L&H and P&C
- The makeup of an insurance company
- How do insurance companies make money?
- How do insurance stocks act?
- Drivers of L&H and P&C
- Insurance regulation

CHARACTERISTICS OF INSURERS

First, what is insurance? An insurance contract is the transfer of risk—a legally binding agreement between an insurer and an insured whereby the insurer will indemnify the insured in exchange for a fee. Insurance spreads risk, sharing the losses of a few among the many. Insurers generally take on certain risks, such as death or accident, in exchange for a fee, referred to as a premium. Premium prices are determined by advanced calculations which attempt to predict the probability and severity of loss. Insurers help the insured mitigate the potential impact of an unforeseen negative event in exchange for a fee from which they expect to overall profit.

Spreading Risk

Insurance spreads risk from the few to the many. Insurers collect premium income from the many and build reserves to cover the losses of the few. Companies often rely on the Law of Large Numbers, which, in the insurance industry, asserts when a large number of people are faced with a low-probability event, the proportion experiencing the event will be close to the mean.

The L&H Insurance sub-industry is the largest in most global insurance benchmarks (Table 4.1). These companies offer insurance for personal and family loss by death, disability, sickness, old age, accident

Table 4.1   Insurance Weights in Major Benchmarks

	World	EAFE	EM	S&P500	R2K
Insurance	**3.8%**	**4.3%**	**2.6%**	**3.6%**	**3.0%**
Insurance Brokers	0.2%	0.0%	0.0%	0.3%	0.1%
Life & Health Insurance	1.3%	1.3%	1.8%	0.9%	0.8%
Multiline Insurance	0.9%	1.6%	0.4%	0.3%	0.1%
Property & Casualty Insurance	1.2%	0.8%	0.4%	2.1%	1.5%
Reinsurance	0.3%	0.5%	0.0%	0.0%	0.6%

Source: Thomson Reuters; S&P 500 and Russell Indexes; MSCI, Inc.[3] As of 12/31/2011.

and unemployment. Products typically include individual annuities, ordinary life insurance, group annuities, group accident and health, other accident and health, group life and others. In 2010, annuities were the largest revenue source in US L&H, with around $346 billion in premiums, or 51% of total premiums.[4] (See Figure 4.1.) Accident & health is the second largest, with about $176 billion, followed by group annuities at about $161 billion.[5]

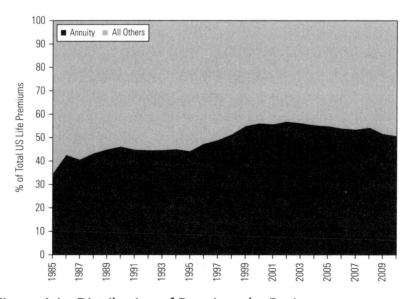

Figure 4.1   Distribution of Premiums by Business
Source: "Understanding Profitability in Life Insurance," *Swiss Re* (January 2012).

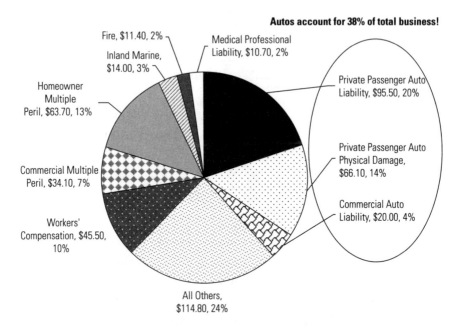

Figure 4.2   2008 US Property and Casualty Premiums (in billions)

Source: AM Best Company, *The Guide to Understanding the Insurance Industry 2009–2010: Check Out the Vital Signs of Financially Fit Insurers* (BookSurge Publishing, October 28, 2009).

Property & Casualty Insurance, the second largest sub-industry in most insurance benchmarks, insures against damages to people or property. This primarily includes auto, homeowner and commercial policies such as workers' compensation (Figure 4.2). The government plays no small role in making these types of policies most prevalent—in many cases, it's the law. While in the US we refer to the industry as Property & Casualty Insurance, or P&C Insurance, outside the US, it's usually called General Insurance.

The Makeup of an Insurance Company

Just like in the banking industry, the makeup of an insurance company's assets and liabilities is a critical component of that company.

Float Cycle

The time between receiving a premium and paying a claim against the policy is considered the "float" cycle. During this period, the insurance company can invest the premium in either the general account or in a separate account.

Assets are mostly composed of bonds, stocks, mortgages and policy loans—which back the insurer's liabilities. In the L&H group, most assets are investments divided between general account and separate account assets. The general account supports contractual obligations with fixed benefit payments (US L&H insurers had general account assets of $3.3 trillion in 2009), while the separate account represents pass-through vehicles such as variable annuities (US L&H insurers had separate account assets of $1.6 trillion in 2009).[6]

Most of the P&C industry's assets are found in the Invested Assets category, which often includes investment categories like short term, equities, fixed and other. In 2011, US P&C companies had $1.4 trillion in assets, with more than 80% classified as "invested assets."[7]

P&C and L&H companies both manage investment portfolios, but the dynamics of the portfolios are often different. Since potential outcomes with P&C insurance are usually shorter term in nature than L&H (in the US, there were 124,000 accidental deaths in 2007, compared to 10.8 million motor vehicle accidents)[8] and catastrophic events usually have more covered property damages than covered deaths, P&C companies typically invest more conservatively—making them less sensitive to trends in capital markets. In fact, as a percent of total assets, L&H companies have considerably more exposure to equities and corporate bonds than P&C. Not only do L&H insurers take on more credit risk by owning more equities or riskier bonds, but they also typically invest in longer-duration securities relative to P&C—which amounts to increased interest rate risk.

Another common asset which can be rather impactful is the *Deferred Policy Acquisition Cost*, or DAC. Since insurance companies incur large upfront expenses upon acquiring new business, such as commissions or policy credits, accounting rules allow insurers to amortize the cost over the policy's life. This deferral accumulates as an asset that is slowly eroded as the expense of the policy is realized over time in the form of Deferred Acquisition Expenses (DAE).

A great way to understand DAC and DAE is to consider an annuity transaction from an insurance company's perspective. Annuities are big money makers for insurance salespeople. They often come with hefty 5%, 6% or 7% commissions on the principal—sometimes more! This means a salesperson could make more than $50,000 selling a million-dollar annuity. In this example, the commission paid would be an expense to the insurance company—an expense the revenue earned from the annuity on day one doesn't come close to matching. So rather than realizing a sizable loss upfront, the insurance company defers the expense over the annuity's life. As more revenue is realized, it releases some of the expense to offset.

Since insurance products' lives and profitability can vary significantly over time, DAC and DAE are based on numerous assumptions—meaning small changes, like a drop in interest rates, for example, can significantly impact DAC calculations and drive earnings deviations.

Liabilities are equally as important as assets. For insurers, liabilities are mostly reserves held to back claims paid to policyholders and beneficiaries. There are several different types of reserves, but policy and asset fluctuation reserves are the most common. Nearly 80% of L&H company liabilities are considered reserves.[9] P&C companies are similarly exposed.

Insurance companies actively manage asset and liability exposures in an effort to control the company's interest rate risk, among other things. These companies usually control the amount of duration mismatch—making sure the interest rate exposures of their assets do not far exceed those of their liabilities, and vice versa. This way, if interest rates move, the company would see a similar impact on both sides.

An insurer's net value is the difference between its assets and liabilities, which also equals its surplus plus its capital stock. Net value is a core metric used in determining an insurer's solvency, which we discuss further in a bit.

HOW DO INSURANCE COMPANIES MAKE MONEY?

Primary revenue sources are:

- Premiums
- Fee income
- Net investment income

L&H and P&C both generate revenue primarily from premiums, fees and investments—all critical components of their profitability.

Insurance is commoditized, and differentiation is slim in the developed world—as a result, insurers can gain market share with either pricing or distribution. Since gaining share with pricing puts the insurer at risk of not earning enough to compensate for claims, distribution is a core way to gain and maintain share. There are a few core distribution platforms: agents, brokers and direct. The most cost-effective platform is offering insurance directly—the insurance company doesn't have to pay commissions to a third party. But agents and brokers can quickly increase an insurer's platform. Bancassurance is a platform where insurance companies and banks partner—the bank offers the insurance company's product via its distribution network, and the commission is shared.

Premiums

The term *premium* refers to the amount the insured pays in exchange for insurance coverage. However, when first collected, only a portion of the premium—the earned premium—will be booked as revenue. Earned premiums funnel down the income statement and contribute to net income for the period.

The remainder is considered *unearned premiums* (UEP)—the portion of the premium not yet earned and parked on the balance sheet as a liability. The liability is reduced as unearned premiums morph into earned premiums and are reflected on the income statement as revenue. The reason for this accounting method is in the event the policy's canceled, the premium would be returned to the insured. However, during the float cycle, it is also considered an asset as it is typically turned into some form of investment.

To see how UEP works, consider a single-pay term life policy. Say the insured purchases a 10-year term life policy and pays a single premium of $1,000 on day one. The insurance company books 10% of that written premium as earned premium in year one, and the remaining $900 represents a liability to the insurer. In year two, it books another $100 in earned premiums, leaving an $800 liability and so on. At the end of year 10, the policy expires and the insurer has no more liability—all income has been earned.

Hard and Soft Markets

The P&C insurance industry is very cyclical, but it is also inelastic since many P&C insurance policies are mandated by law. As such, the cyclical nature is not tied to the economic cycle, but to an underwriting cycle.

Like most insurance, P&C insurance is mostly commoditized—so the most important factor for most customers is price.[10] It also has low barriers to entry. These two dynamics create an underwriting cycle which generally drives "hard market" or "soft market" conditions.

During a "soft market," prices are low or falling, which results in falling underwriting standards as companies compete for market share. Ultimately, either prices or underwriting standards fall too much, leading in turn to losses. As these losses mount, some companies shut their doors, and eventually, supply is reduced enough to restore the market's pricing power.

In a "hard market," insurance companies have pricing power, which typically leads to higher profitability. This in turn attracts new players to the market in pursuit of profit. Eventually, this turns into oversupply, and the soft market cycle starts anew. (See Figure 4.3.)

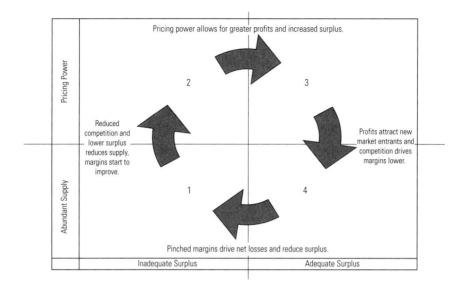

Figure 4.3   P&C Underwriting Cycle

Hard markets are often event-driven. Consider a hurricane's impact during a soft market: The catastrophe would drive substantial covered losses, and the industry would likely witness insolvent insurers, given already low underwriting standards and pricing. Following the event, demand for insurance would surge as people are reminded of its benefits, but supply would have dwindled, leading to hard market conditions where the remaining insurers would have pricing power and benefit from the increased demand at higher prices.

Earnings from premium income are typically referred to as *underwriting income*. A common measure of underwriting income is the *combined ratio*, which combines the *loss ratio* and the *expense ratio*. The *loss ratio* measures incurred losses and loss-adjustment expenses to earned premiums. The *expense ratio* measures incurred expenses to earned premiums. So the *combined ratio* measures losses plus expenses to premiums—essentially, the profitability of the underwriting side of the business.

A combined ratio of 100% means the insurance written is equivalent to losses and expenses incurred, excluding any gains or losses on investments. A ratio above 100% means the insurer is losing money writing insurance; below 100% means its underwriting business is profitable.

But a ratio above 100% does not mean the company as a whole is losing money—in fact, an insurer can run its underwriting at a loss for extended time periods, provided it's making money on its investment portfolio (see Figure 4.4). Since the P&C market is highly penetrated in the developed world, competition is fierce—insurance companies usually price their policy pools very close to expected loss payouts. In fact, from 1980 to 2006, US P&C insurance companies recorded underwriting profits in only two years.[11]

Loss Ratio: Losses/Earned Premiums

+

Expense Ratio: Expenses/Earned Premiums

=

Combined Ratio: (Losses + Expenses)/Earned Premiums

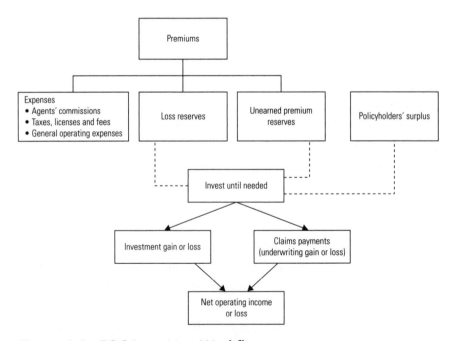

Figure 4.4   P&C Insurance Workflow

Investment Income

Investment portfolios also provide another important income source in the form of dividends, interest and gains or losses on securities (as with any portfolio). Insurance companies are some of the largest institutional investors in the world, with over $6 trillion in US insurer investments alone.

Since most of an insurance company's expenses are accounted for on the underwriting side of the business (combined ratio), most gains or losses on the investment portfolio go directly to the bottom line. Understanding an insurer's investment portfolio is an important step to investing in an insurance company. Finding an insurer with an investment portfolio positioned to benefit from your market expectations could give you a leg up.

Fee Income

Globally, insurance companies manage nearly $25 trillion.[12] This makes investment management a huge component of fee income, primarily for L&H insurers, and means L&H companies are directly impacted by asset and savings trends (see Chapter 3). Again, if you can find an insurer that manages assets you expect to outperform, this could put it at an advantage to its peers if your forecasts play out.

When Non-Premium Income Adds Up

If an insurer makes an excess return on its investment portfolio or earns excess income from fees, it may sometimes use this revenue to improve its insurance business. For example, it could afford lower pricing on insurance products, thereby possibly capturing more market share. As with most things, though, extremes can be bad—beware an insurance company underpricing risk in an effort to gain share.

Expenses

The largest expense for an insurance company is usually policyholder claims, or paying out on insured losses. Insurance companies expect these expenses—they're a core component of pricing in the sense they'll generally price their policies in an effort to turn a profit despite an expected amount in losses on a pool of insurance contracts. This is similar to banks' pricing loans partly based on expected losses on a pool of loans.

The next largest expense is generally amortization of deferred costs and expenses. Other notable expenses include commissions, salaries, legal fees and other overhead, not unlike expenses witnessed in non-financial sectors.

HOW DO INSURANCE COMPANIES ACT?

As could be expected, Insurance industries are positively correlated to the broader Financials sector. However, Insurance Brokers tends to be lower beta, has a lower correlation than the other industries and is less volatile when measured using standard deviation.

Brokers is typically referred to as the more "defensive" component of Insurance because whereas the other sub-industries may pay out large claims, insurance brokerages simply sell the other sub-industries' insurance products, so there's no event risk. On the contrary, if a hurricane hits Florida, Brokers could benefit as demand for protection from the next hurricane increases, but the P&C or Multiline insurers would likely take substantial losses due to the event. Insurance brokers also typically don't have investment portfolios, making them less susceptible to (positive or negative) capital markets trends.

The Multiline industry has the highest beta, the highest correlation to the Financials sector and the highest standard deviation. However, the primary reason for that is stock-specific issues during 2008's financial panic (Table 4.2). In particular, American International Group's (AIG) rise, fall and subsequent government bailout tied to its exposures to derivatives and various guarantees greatly skew the data. In fact, prior to its downfall, AIG was the single largest component of the S&P 500 Insurance Index—at one point accounting for more than 30% of the group.[13] Analyzing the group prior to 2008 shows a more muted variance, but the general trends remain.

Table 4.2   Insurance Sub-Industry: Beta & Correlation to the Financials Sector and Standard Deviation of Returns

	Beta	Correlation	Standard Deviation
Multi-Line	1.30	0.93	39.9%
Life & Health	0.91	0.84	30.4%
Property & Casualty	0.70	0.83	23.7%
Insurance Brokers	0.45	0.57	21.8%

Source: Thomson Reuters; S&P 500 Indexes, monthly data from 12/31/1995 to 12/31/2011.

The general relationship between the industries can be summed up by ranking them by volatility or sensitivity to economic conditions: Multiline is the most volatile, followed by L&H, then P&C and finally Brokers. This ranking holds up through most economic cycles—whether employment, interest rates, inflation, recessions, expansions, bulls or bears.

Drivers

Insurance growth rates tend to go hand-in-hand with economic activity and the growth in economic wealth. The more activity and the more wealth, the more insurance (Figure 4.5). This is magnified in frontier and Emerging Markets, since there's a threshold where insurance becomes widely accepted—a threshold the developed world passed decades ago. Developed markets are rather penetrated, so growing much more than an economy's growth rate becomes a fight for market share—as laid out in the market cycle discussion.

In the developing world, growth is still robust. Not only are economic growth rates overall higher, but as nations become wealthier, there's a tipping point where an economy is wealthy enough to support an insurance market. P&C insurance can be supported earlier on in the growth cycle, but it takes per-capita GDP of around $8,000 before a local life insurance market can be sustained.[14]

Regardless of geography, following are a few high-level drivers influencing the industry globally.

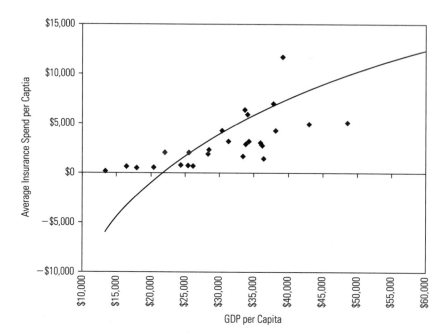

Figure 4.5   Economic Wealth Versus Insurance Spending by Country

Source: Organisation for Economic Co-operation and Development, "Total Gross Insurance Premiums," 2010; Thomson Reuters, as of 12/31/2011.

Life and Health

The L&H group tends to be sensitive to savings trends, asset values and interest rates. Moreover, considering the importance of annuities, an understanding of drivers there is important.

> **Savings trends:** Since insurance companies are such large asset managers and many of their products are savings oriented, personal savings trends are important. Savings trends can dictate investment flow into annuities or insurance accounts.
>
> **Value of assets:** If asset values are rising, not only do portfolio values rise, but insurers receive more management fees. Investors may get a better idea of which companies are better positioned by examining their portfolios.

Interest rates: Interest rates impact many components of an insurance company. Higher rates can increase investment income, widen spreads on products and increase volumes, while lower rates can have the opposite impact. Equally important, swings in interest rates can impact DAC calculations.

Annuities: An individual annuity is an insurance product set up to make periodic payments to individuals for a specific time period, often over an individual's lifetime. These products can be single premium or multiple premiums, variable or fixed, immediate or deferred. All annuities grow on a tax-deferred basis. Group annuities can be similar, but instead of one investor's expected time horizon, they take the entire group into consideration.

For insurance companies, offering annuities and life insurance is a calculated bet based on mortality tables. With life insurance, companies would prefer the insured live as long as possible to extend premium payments and/or expense income. With annuities, companies would prefer shorter life spans so annuity payments end sooner rather than later.

A big distinction in the annuity space is fixed versus variable. Fixed annuities offer payments at a fixed interest rate which is not tied to the stock market but could be adjusted based on certain interest rate benchmarks. A variable annuity typically offers a range of investment options—many of which are tied to investing in stocks or bonds. Fixed annuities tend to sell better in periods of uncertainty—not unlike bonds, which are also typically more popular during bear markets. Conversely, variable annuities sell better during bull markets—when investor confidence is improving.

Variable annuities often offer some sort of guarantee on principal—they allow investors market exposure but with some sort of insurance on the portfolio. These guarantees earn enormous fees for the annuity companies, but during a market downturn, they can be disastrous because the insurers may be held liable for insured investor losses.

During 2008–2009's financial crisis, they pushed many to the brink of insolvency.

Property and Casualty

Considering the typically saturated nature of property and casualty insurance and the prevalence of automobile insurance, general economic growth (i.e., GDP and population growth) and automobile trends are core drivers of the group. However, since insurance is a business of risk, unexpected catastrophes can easily change things.

> **Economic growth**: A core driver behind P&C insurance premium growth is simply economic growth. As an economy grows, demand for P&C insurance grows along with it at a clip of about 1.3x.[15]
>
> **Auto insurance:** Since auto insurance is such a huge part of P&C (Figure 4.2), it's important to pay attention to trends in that segment of the market. Increased automobile sales aside, things like interest rates, sentiment, disposable income trends and the automobile fleet's age are driving factors in the developed world. In Emerging Markets, a core driver is per-capita income—as countries become wealthier, they can afford more luxury items such as automobiles.
>
> **Catastrophic loss:** Catastrophic losses can drive insurance company losses but can also create a hard market, which can be good for the industry.

REGULATION

As with the other Financials industry groups, the government plays a huge role in insurance—from regulation mandating compulsory coverage to licensing requirements and regulation controlling how much risk an insurance company can take, regulation can have a measurable impact. Globally, regulation isn't that different—regulators generally provide a framework within which insurance companies must operate. The framework can differ around the world, but it is usually rather robust, covering everything from competition to disclosure to cross-border cooperation. However, nearly all regulatory regimes include some form of leverage and/or risk controls. In doing so, there are some common metrics used to ensure soundness and solvency in the industry.

Ratios

In the US, individual states determine capital levels required to be considered solvent. While not all of these are used by all regulators, following are a few common ratios.

> **Solvency ratio:** The solvency ratio is a measure of an insurance company's obligations versus its capital, or its leverage—specifically its net assets/net premiums written.
>
> **Capital ratio:** A common ratio in the L&H industry, which is capital as a percentage of general account assets.
>
> **Risk-based capital (RBC) ratio:** Risk-based capital is calculated via complicated models based on the risk of an insurer's exposures. In the RBC ratio, RBC is the denominator and total capital is the numerator. For regulatory purposes, the ratio is doubled in the US (we didn't make this up). The National Association of Insurance Commissioners (NAIC) suggests insurance companies have an RBC ratio greater than 200%—if it drops below 200%, regulators may take action; if it drops below 70%, regulators may take over the insurer altogether.
>
> **Net leverage:** The sum of a company's net premium written and net liabilities to policyholder surplus.
>
> **Premium-to-surplus ratio:** The ratio of written premiums to surplus, typically used for P&C insurers to measure leverage.

Credit Ratings

Insurance is only as good as the entity providing it—so insurers' credit ratings are important. A high credit rating can give the perception of safety and allow for lower borrowing costs and better pricing in certain markets. It can also open up other markets, such as when certain regulatory schemes or potential customers have a mandated

(Continued)

minimum credit rating. When determining a credit rating, most Nationally Recognized Statistical Rating Organizations (NRSROs), such as Moody's or Fitch, review an insurer's capital level as a core part of the rating process.

US Regulation

The US insurance industry has historically been regulated by a state-based regulatory regime, although many additional regulatory bodies now take part under Dodd-Frank. Each state has an insurance commissioner assisted by the National Association of Insurance Commissioners (NAIC), which is a voluntary organization of chief state insurance regulators. The NAIC's mission is protecting policyholders, claimants and beneficiaries first and foremost while also facilitating an effective and efficient marketplace. The NAIC also monitors and enforces seven financial solvency core principles:

1. Regulatory reporting, disclosure and transparency
2. Off-site monitoring and analysis
3. On-site risk-focused examinations
4. Reserves, capital adequacy and solvency
5. Regulatory control of significant, broad-based, risk-related transactions and activities
6. Preventive and corrective measures, including enforcement
7. Exiting the market and receivership

For now, each state can interpret, enact and enforce its interpretation of these principles as it sees fit—though Dodd-Frank may eventually move toward a national regulatory body.

Solvency II (Europe)

Solvency II is a full-scale revision of the solvency framework and prudential regime applicable to insurance and reinsurance companies. It was adopted November 2009, and each state in the European Economic Area (EEA) is required to implement Solvency II by

January 2013. The European Commission developed Solvency II using a three-pillar approach in an effort to unify a single European Union insurance market while also implementing a more risk-sensitive and sophisticated solvency requirement.

> Pillar I: Quantitative Requirements: *Introduces economic risk-based solvency requirements—namely, the solvency capital requirement and the minimum capital requirement*
>
> Pillar II: Supervisory Requirements: *Introduces a supervisory review process and strengthens regulatory supervision*
>
> Pillar III: Disclosure Requirements: *Demands more disclosure*

At the time of this writing, the core ruling on required capital levels under Pillar I is still unknown. Insurance companies in Europe have been making progress in implementing the new rules, but as with Basel III, the rules are still being written and are subject to change.

The International Association of Insurance Supervisors

The International Association of Insurance Supervisors provides the *Insurance Core Principles* (ICPs), which is a globally accepted framework for the supervision of the insurance sector. The principles are similar to the US core principles but are more numerous—at last count, there are 26 ICPs, ranging from maintaining a clearly defined supervisor to cooperating during cross-border crises.[16]

5

REAL ESTATE INDUSTRY GROUP

Whuen people think about real estate, most may think first of residential real estate—whether a single-family home in the suburbs or a condo by the beach. This category includes one- to four-unit properties, and while the sheer size and breadth of the market make pinpointing the true value difficult, it's safe to say it's one of the largest markets in the world.

When it comes to equity investing, real estate typically refers to commercial property designed for retail, wholesale, office, hotel or service use, which globally accounts for more than $21 trillion in assets.[1] It also refers to residential real estate in excess of four units, such as apartment buildings or senior living facilities. Companies focused on commercial properties are in the Real Estate Industry group.

The Real Estate Industry group is the smallest in the Financials sector in most major indexes, with one exception—US small-cap benchmarks. The group consists of Real Estate Investment Trusts (REITs) and Real Estate Management & Development (REMD) companies, both of which concern owning, managing, financing and/or developing mostly commercial real estate assets. It represents 2.6%

of the MSCI World index, with most REIT exposure in the US, while most Management & Development companies are outside the US (Table 5.1).[2]

Table 5.1   Real Estate Industry Group Weight in Major Benchmarks

	World	EAFE	EM	S&P 500	FR2000
Real Estate	2.6%	3.0%	1.6%	1.9%	8.2%
Real Estate Investment Trusts—REITs	*1.8%*	*1.4%*	*0.0%*	*1.8%*	*8.1%*
Real Estate Management & Development	*0.8%*	*1.7%*	*1.6%*	*0.0%*	*0.1%*

Source: Thomson Reuters; S&P 500 and Russell 2000 Indexes; MSCI, Inc.[3] As of 12/31/2011.

Since REITs dominate the Real Estate Industry and are similar globally, this chapter primarily focuses on the US REIT industry. We discuss:

- What is a REIT?
- Equity, mortgage or hybrid?
- REIT characteristics
- REITs in detail
- Common REIT terms

Small Cap REITS

As noted, within US small-cap benchmarks, Real Estate has a much larger presence, thanks to REITs. This is because the typical REIT has a market capitalization of just $600 million and is relatively US-centric.[4]

A commonly used benchmark for US small-cap companies is the Russell 2000. Within this index, the Real Estate Industry group accounts for over 8% of the benchmark—38% of total Financials exposure.[5] This exposure is primarily REITs, but there's a smattering of other companies in the index.

WHAT IS A REIT?

A REIT is an investment fund focused on real estate assets that comingles investor funds to purchase primarily commercial properties and mortgages. REITs were created to allow broad access to investment opportunities in diversified, professionally managed real estate enterprises. While REITs vary globally, each type's core rules are typically the same—to qualify as a REIT (regardless of type or nationality), a company typically must have most of its assets and income tied directly to commercial real estate assets and distribute most of its earnings to shareholders. These rules were established to make REITs as similar as possible to owning real estate assets directly and are a precondition for favorable tax treatment.

A Bit of History

REITs came to be through the Cigar Excise Tax Extension of 1960, passed by Congress and signed by President Dwight D. Eisenhower, in an effort to offer average Americans the opportunity to invest in diversified portfolios of professionally managed commercial real estate assets—something previously accessible only to the wealthy or institutions. REITs' special federal tax treatment was designed to make REIT ownership similar to direct property ownership.

In 1969, the Netherlands passed REIT (or REIT-like) legislation, sparking gradual REIT globalization. The Netherlands (1969) and Australia (1985) aside, it wasn't until the 2000s that REITs really became popular worldwide—68% of countries with REIT-like legislation adopted it in the twenty-first century, including Japan (2001), France (2003), Germany (2007) and the UK (2007). As of March 2012, 28 countries have publicly traded REITs.

Investable REITs

REITs can be categorized as publicly traded, public non-listed or private entities (Table 5.2). Whereas publicly traded REITs trade like stocks (typically on an exchange) and are available to the masses, public non-listed and private REITs cater to longer-term investors and typically have higher minimum investments and a potentially opaque liquidation process. Since we are examining REITs as they relate to equity investing, we will focus on publicly traded REITs.

Table 5.2   Types and Characteristics of REITs

	Publicly Traded	Public Non-Listed	Private
Structure	Registered with SEC and trade on a stock exchange.	Registered with the SEC but not traded on an exchange.	Not registered and not traded on an exchange.
Liquidity	Shares trade like a stock; transaction costs are similar to stocks.	Redemption programs vary but are typically limited. Often there is a required liquidation date and a minimum holding period.	Typically illiquid; varies by company.
Management	Typically self-managed and advised, with majority of directors being independent.	Typically externally managed and advised, with majority of directors being independent.	Typically externally managed, with no board requirements.
Corporate Governance & Disclosures	Follow stock exchange rules, required to make regular financial disclosures.	Follow NASAA regulations, must make regular financial disclosures.	n/a

Source: "Which Type of REIT Is Right for You?" NAREIT (2009).

UpREIT or DownREIT?

REITs commonly use partnerships in various ways. In this regard, there are three basic REIT structures: a traditional REIT, an Umbrella Partnership REIT (UPREIT) and the DownREIT. The type of REIT is important to understand as it affects ownership structure and consequently financial reporting, but ultimately a REIT is a REIT, and they will act similarly regardless of structure.

Taxes

REITs receive beneficial tax treatment at the corporate level—meaning provided certain rules are met, REITs don't pay income tax. This makes REIT ownership pretty similar to direct property ownership. Without this tax treatment, REIT dividends would typically be taxed at the corporate and investor levels, compared to owning property directly, which is typically taxed only at the investor level.

There are different types of REIT dividends, the most common being an ordinary dividend, based on normal operations (E&P, or earnings and profits) from rental, lease, dividend or interest income. These dividends are generally taxed as ordinary income to individual REIT investors and typically account for the majority of dividends. REITs can also distribute dividends in the form of capital gains, return of capital or deprecation recoveries, which would likely be taxed differently. Interested investors should consult a tax expert for further clarification of these differences.

Equity, Mortgage or Hybrid?

REITs are broken down into three categories: equity REIT, mortgage REIT or hybrid REIT. Equity REITs typically invest directly in commercial properties, whereas mortgage REITs typically invest in mortgages or other debt instruments related to commercial properties. Hybrid REITs invest in both—since they're less common, they're often categorized as either equity or mortgage REITs, depending on their primary focus. Globally, 92% of REITs are equity and 8% are mortgage.[6]

There are seven sub-industries in the REIT Industry, each focusing on a different area of real estate: Diversified, Industrial, Mortgage, Office, Residential, Retail and Specialized (Table 5.3).

The Retail sub-industry is the largest in global benchmarks, while Specialized is the largest in domestic benchmarks—driven primarily by storage and hotels.

Table 5.3   REIT Sub-Industries as a % of the REIT Industry

Sub-Industries	MSCI World	MSCI EAFE	MSCI EM	S&P 500	Russell 2000
Diversified REITs	15%	31%		7%	8%
Industrial REITs	6%	7%		6%	6%
Mortgage REITs	4%				17%
Office REITs	9%	54%		7%	11%
Residential REITs	7%		100%	15%	15%
Retail REITs	36%	0%		21%	17%
Specialized REITs	24%			43%	26%

Source: Thomson Reuters; S&P 500 and Russell 2000 Indexes; MSCI, Inc.[7] As of 12/31/2011.

REIT CHARACTERISTICS

There are numerous ways to describe REITs, but a few core characteristics stand out: REITs are *value* and *small*, pay *dividends* and are defensive-ish and impacted by interest rates. Furthermore, as with all securities, REITs and the underlying properties are driven by supply and demand.

REITs Are Value

Growth investors tend to favor companies with above-average earnings growth rates, while value investors tend to prefer companies with below-average valuations. There are many benchmarks for each style, including the well-known Russell Value and Growth Indexes. REITs, with normally low growth rates, higher dividend yields and below-average valuations, are typically preferred by value investors.

REITs Are Small

Historically, big companies fare better during recessions because they're seen as relative safe havens, while small companies bounce big early in recoveries because they've usually suffered more during the preceding recession and bounce bigger off the bottom. And since REITs are usually small, it's no surprise they typically perform better when small cap is beating large cap.

Dividends

Since REITs are required to distribute at least 90% of income to share-holders, REIT dividend yields are generally higher than the market, making dividends a core component of REIT investing. Since REITs' inception, dividends have generally accounted for all cumulative total return—price swings up and down have mostly offset each other.

Dividends and Taxes

One of the most important factors in determining dividends' value is tax policy. Dividends may be taxed at a different rate from normal income or long-term capital gains. When tax rates change, it could materially affect dividends' value relative to other forms of income. Further, tax policy can influence whether a firm chooses to pay a dividend and how much. Though investors have different tax situations, REITs' US tax treatment is one consideration.

Supply and Demand

Commercial property demand can be volatile, ebbing and flow-ing with the economic cycle, but supply is more stable and easier to quantify. Property supply can be measured a few ways: absorption rates, vacancies, new construction, permits and construction spend-ing, all of which are well reported and commonly updated monthly (Figure 5.1). Considering REITs typically have a limited geo-graphic presence and in real estate it is mostly about "LOCATION, LOCATION, LOCATION," understanding supply and demand trends for the underlying property market is critical when investing in REITs.

Property Prices

Physical property prices are a core component of REIT valua-tions, though REITs tend to *lead* property prices (see Table 5.4 and Figure 5.2). This relationship exists because of the liquid nature of exchange-traded REITs and the illiquid nature of physical properties. Markets react to new information quickly, and since you can buy or sell many REITs with the click of a button, they tend to react quicker. While this drives the leading nature of REITs, it also adds to the vola-tility relative to physical property prices.

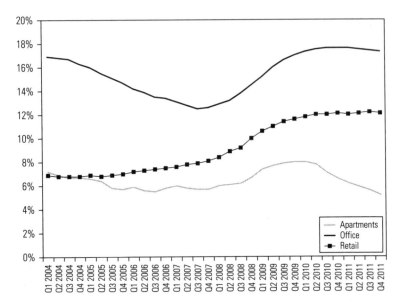

Figure 5.1   US Vacancy Rates 2004–2011

Source: Thomson Reuters, Reis 12/31/2004–12/31/2011.

Table 5.4   Correlation of NCREIF TBI National Property Index and the NAREIT All REIT Index

	Correlation
4Q Lead	**0.52**
3Q Lead	0.50
2Q Lead	0.42
1Q Lead	0.29
Concurrent	0.14
1Q Lag	−0.02
2Q Lag	−0.15
3Q Lag	−0.22
4Q Lag	−0.25

Source: National Council of Real Estate Investment Fiduciaries; Thomson Reuters from 12/31/1977 to 12/31/2011.

REITs Are Defensive-ish

Since the NAREIT US REIT Index's 1971 inception, REITs have tended to be defensive. When the S&P 500 is negative on a total-return basis over a 12-month period, it averages −15%—during

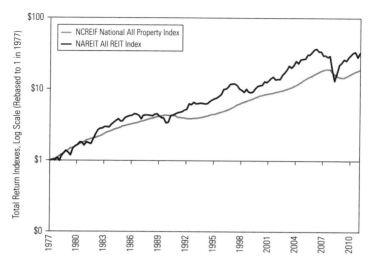

Figure 5.2   Growth of a Dollar (Moody's TBI Property Index Versus NAREIT REIT Index)

Source: National Council of Real Estate Investment Fiduciaries, Moody's, Thomson Reuters. From 12/31/1977 to 12/31/2011.

the same periods, REITs average –6%. However, when the S&P 500 is positive in 12 months, it averages 19%, while REITs average 17%.[8] Simply, REITs tend to underperform when the market rises and outperform when the market falls. By no means does this ensure REITs will underperform during every bull market or outperform during every bear—but it has been the case on average.

REITs Are Interest-Rate Sensitive

REITs are interest-rate sensitive in two very important ways: If interest rates fall, it could make financing a property cheaper, which could increase REITs' profitability. Additionally, since REITs distribute dividends, rising interest rates could make other cash-flowing investments more attractive if a given REIT doesn't increase its dividend.

REITs in Detail—Mortgage and Equity REITs

Mortgage and equity REITs are impacted by different drivers and act differently over time. Whereas equity REITs are impacted by commercial property trends, mortgage REITs are impacted by residential housing credit markets.

Mortgage REITs

A mortgage REIT, or mREIT, specializes in mortgages and mortgage-backed securities (MBS), both residential and commercial. These mortgages can be purchased from third parties, or the mREIT can underwrite the loans directly—either way, it functions primarily as a pool of mortgage-backed securities. Whereas an equity REIT can be viewed as a mutual funds of real estate assets, mREITs can be viewed as mutual funds of mutual funds of mortgages. While the focus of mREITs is mortgages, domestically, they own a very small slice of the overall mortgage and MBS pie.

Mortgage-Backed Securities (MBS)

A mortgage-backed security (MBS), in its purest form, is simply a pool of mortgages lumped together into a single security. In the US, there are two general types of residential mortgage-backed securities: agency MBS and private-label MBS. Agency MBS are those conforming to underwriting rules set out by US government agencies such as Federal Home Loan Mortgage Corporation (Freddie Mac), Federal National Mortgage Association (Fannie Mae) or Government National Mortgage Association (Ginnie Mae) and are guaranteed by the agency accordingly. Private-label MBS have no underlying underwriting rules and are therefore considered much riskier than their agency brethren. The vast majority of MBS are agency MBS. The 2008 financial crisis all but shut down the private-label MBS market due to poor underwriting standards earlier in the decade—and proposed regulation puts this market further at risk.

A REPRESENTATIVE EXAMPLE: ANNALY CAPITAL MANAGEMENT

As of December 2011, Annaly Capital (NLY) is the largest US mortgage REIT—its $15.5 billion market capitalization nearly doubles its nearest peer and accounts for about 35% of total mortgage REIT market capitalization.[9] Moreover, it accounts for 36% of total mortgage REIT assets.[10] Since NLY is such a dominant presence, let's take a look at what makes it tick.

At the heart of a mortgage REIT is its portfolio of mortgages. NLY's $104 billion MBS portfolio accounts for 95% of its total assets.[11] Of this, 100% is considered agency—underwritten per Freddie, Fannie or Ginnie guidelines. This puts its portfolio at little risk of a credit event—unless the agencies themselves were to default.

Since NLY is essentially a leveraged pool of agency MBS, it's important to note the direct link between NLY and agency MBS. Figure 5.3 clearly illustrates Mortgage REITs' relationship to a benchmark agency MBS index.

Looking at the NAREIT mREIT index shows a similar pattern (Figure 5.4), with some noticeable differences. Note the relationship between mREITs and agency bonds fell apart around 2003 and then again in the 2007–2008 period. In the early part of the decade, private-label MBS outperformed agency MBS, and mREITs benefited from

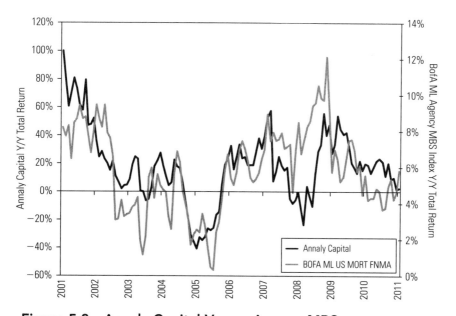

Figure 5.3   Annaly Capital Versus Agency MBS
Source: Bank of America Merrill Lynch, Thomson Reuters from 12/31/2000 to 12/31/2011.

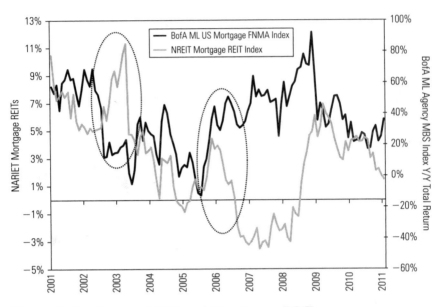

Figure 5.4   Agency MBS and Mortgage REITs

Source: Bank of America Merrill Lynch, Thomson Reuters from December 2000 to December 2011.

exposure to the riskier mortgages. Then, later in the decade, agency MBS vastly outperformed as mortgages started to sour. During this time, many mREITs went bankrupt or were dissolved. However, the relationship between Annaly Capital and agency bonds stayed pretty tight during this time, primarily due to its focus on agency MBS.

As you can tell, the type of MBS within the portfolio makes all the difference—credit risk is a big concern for private label, less so for agencies.

If mREITs Act Like MBS, Then What Drives MBS' Total Return?

Interest rates' direction, interest-rate spreads, the number of pre-payments and the potential for credit events (defaults) impact MBS returns. Simply put, rising interest rates, wider spreads, increased pre-payments or increased default expectations could all pressure MBS values. A firm understanding of these drivers is imperative when investing in mREITs—allowing investors to over- or underweight appropriately and providing guidance on which characteristics likely play a role moving forward.

EQUITY REIT SUB-INDUSTRIES

Each equity REIT sub-industry focuses on a particular real estate sector and has unique characteristics over and above the aforementioned shared traits.

Retail REITs

Retail REITs focus primarily on leasing properties to retail-oriented companies, such as grocery or electronics stores or even regional malls or outlet centers—meaning they tend to be more tied to consumer spending patterns than the others.

Rent is a core revenue source and is typically broken into minimum rent and overage rent—the minimum rent typically tied to inflation and overage rent tied to tenants' sales. As tenants' sales improve, so does the rent, and vice versa.

Location, Location, Location!

Regardless of which sub-industry a REIT falls into, location is key as it determines supply and demand, growth rates, barriers to entry, employment trends, capital spending patterns, general economic activity, pricing, employee stock and even cost of capital … nearly everything! Better locations are typically reflected in better (higher) REIT values—some REITs trade at premium multiples because they are in high-barrier areas. For example, a residential REIT may own properties in exclusive neighborhoods, an office REIT may own a large section of a major central business district (CBD) or an industrial REIT may own properties adjacent to every major airport in the nation. These are characteristics, and possibly advantages, some REITs have. But consider this is typically widely known information, meaning the REIT premium may overstate the REIT's true value. As with most industries, REITs are subject to legislative risk (among others)—if politicians decide to convert some attractive open space in a luxury residential area to heavy industrial space, the REIT premium would likely disappear near-instantaneously.

Office REITs

Office REITs own and operate office properties and earn revenue primarily from office rents. Leases are among the longest, with

7- to 10-year leases not unheard of, making office REITs less cyclical than others. If market rents move lower, it takes longer for that decrease to impact office REITs since most leases are "locked in." Similarly, in robust economic times, office REITs are at a disadvantage to those able to quickly increase rents. This is why office REITs typically offer information on "above-market" and "below-market" rents and lease expiration schedules. If a REIT is heavy on "above-market" rents and has many leases expiring soon, this may lead to reduced upcoming rental income as those rents are either adjusted down or lost completely if tenants move. Of course, the reverse could also happen.

Occupancy or Rent Trade-Off?

Be cognizant of what is driving occupancy gains—sometimes REITs lower rental rates just to establish higher occupancy. This is a fine strategy, but if it goes too far, the REIT could risk being considered lower quality due to below-market rents. If the REIT has established itself as a quality name, this could have negative implications.

Building quality is an important consideration in analyzing office REITs' portfolios. Buildings are generally classified into three grades referring to property quality: Classes A, B and C. Class A properties are the highest quality, Class B are mid-quality and Class C are the lowest quality.

Beyond portfolio quality, tenancy is of utmost importance. Major office space users are legal services, other financial companies such as banks and insurance companies, professional services, the government and affiliated agencies and health care companies. Office REITs often focus on a particular niche, which can make the REIT act differently from more diversified REITs, so understanding tenant industry trends is crucial. For example, in adverse economic times, a focus on government contracts may be prudent because occupancy trends here are typically more stable.

Residential REITs

Residential REITs focus on residential properties, including multi-family homes, apartments, manufactured homes and student housing properties. An important distinction is the residential properties owned by residential REITs are commercial interests—i.e., the properties are cash flow-generating properties, typically not single-family residences.

Home ownership is Residential REITs' main competition. Residential REITs prefer an environment where mortgage affordability and interest rates are low. This way, the REIT can access cheap funding while consumers cannot afford to buy, so they rent—driving up aggregate demand for space in their properties and making the REIT quite profitable. If affordability improves, more renters can afford to purchase and vacancies could increase as rental demand falls. Additionally, rising interest rates could pinch profitability—but they would also likely pressure home affordability through increased mortgage rates. Understanding the cost of owning versus the cost of renting is useful in considering residential REITs.

Likewise, residential REITs will be impacted by renters' and owners' considerations, such as job growth, government program changes, etc.

Industrial REITs

Industrial REITs focus on properties that are used primarily for logistics, operations such as transport, distribution, packing or storage. Industrial properties can be simple warehouses or complex distribution facilities, but regardless, they are typically found close to major arterial road, air and/or sea networks. Since many industrial buildings are relatively inexpensive to build, supply is more fluid than many other types of properties. Think of a simple warehouse—there's not much to it.

As the name implies, industrial activity drives demand for these types of properties, as does global trade.

Diversified REITs

A diversified REIT is generally focused on a combination of office, retail and/or residential properties. Aspects of each sub-industry impact diversifieds, but the diversified REIT may benefit from synergies among the groups. An office REIT could develop a project where its core is office buildings, but it supplements these offices with a smattering of retail shops and apartments to capture as much demand as possible.

Specialized REITs

Specialized REITs are typically those without sufficient company representation to warrant a specific sub-industry classification. Core areas in specialized REITs include health care, hotel and storage. Whereas hotel and storage REITs tend to be more economically sensitive due to very short lease duration, health care's generally longer lease structure makes it a bit less so.

UNIQUE MEASUREMENTS FOR REITs

Because traditional GAAP accounting rules don't really work for REITs, the industry focuses on funds from operations (FFO) instead of earnings and on net asset value (NAV) instead of book value. The industry also uses cap rate for property valuations and net operating income (NOI) for core profitability measurements.

Funds From Operations (FFO)

FFO, the most common measure of a REIT's operation performance, is generally defined as net income excluding gains (or losses) from property sales plus depreciation and amortization and after adjustments for unconsolidated partnerships and joint ventures. The aim is producing a measure of consolidated operating performance that's repeatable and avoids the drawbacks of using historical cost depreciation. Since real estate assets don't typically rise or fall predictably over time like other assets such as machinery, computer software or inventory, historical cost depreciation is considered inappropriate for REITs, and FFO is a way to measure performance excluding depreciation and amortization.

Because FFO is usually considered to portray REIT growth, strength and valuations, the price-to-FFO ratio (P/FFO) could be considered the industry's equivalent of the price-to-earnings (P/E) ratio. Inverting the P/FFO gives you an FFO yield, which can be considered equivalent to a company's earnings yield. It's important to keep in mind, though, an FFO yield cannot effectively be compared to a company in another industry's earnings yield. In fact, FFO yields are generally best restricted to individual sub-industries within REITs.

Net Asset Value (NAV)

NAV measures a REIT's value, typically in terms of assets minus liabilities—with some adjustments. This is similar (but not equivalent) to book value since, as with FFO, REITs are skewed by considerable depreciation of their real estate assets. NAV uses the fair value of these assets rather than cost minus depreciation.

Because REITs are much more liquid than most real estate assets, REITs' market capitalizations typically move before the value of the underlying assets. If investors believe the REIT's portfolio is more valuable than recent NAV valuations, investors may drive the market capitalization above the REIT's NAV.

Liquidity Premium

Due to REITs' more liquid nature, they often have an associated liquidity premium relative to property prices—investors are generally willing to pay more for a more liquid investment. This is another reason REITs can trade at a premium to underlying property values.

Net Operating Income (NOI)

NOI is the company's (continuing) operating income minus (continuing) operating expenses—it excludes one-time or extraordinary events.

Because depreciation and amortization skew net income and since FFO is an adjusted number, net operating income (NOI) is a measurement often used to report the status of a REIT's operations. Moreover, NOI is used in determining cap rates and NAV, so it is useful in many ways.

Cap Rates

A cap rate, or capitalization rate, is simply net operating income divided by property value. Said another way, a cap rate can be considered the profitability level of a property or portfolio of properties. One problem with cap rates is they rely on property values, which can be rather arbitrarily determined and based on myriad assumptions and variables, like expected rents, cost of funds, risk premiums and other projections. However, cap rates can be useful for comparison purposes, provided the same methodology's used over time.

As with any ratio, rising cap rates can signal rising NOI, or they can equally mean falling property prices—the driver behind the trend is important.

Forward implied cap rates can be used as a proxy for cap rates, which can fluctuate widely. The forward implied rate uses NOI divided by enterprise value and attempts to discern a cap rate based on current market expectations. Enterprise value is essentially market capitalization plus net debt and is often referred to as a theoretical takeover value, since this would be the total cost of acquiring the property at current market pricing. Since enterprise value and NOI are given items, this takes some of the guesswork out of REIT analysis.

Pro Forma Cap Rates

When reviewing a REIT's or property's stated cap rate, pay attention to whether it's pro forma. *Pro forma* refers to what is expected to happen, rather than what actually happened today or just happened last quarter. If you see a pro forma cap rate, try to determine how far in the future the analysis is projecting, and use your own judgment to determine whether this is reasonable or not.

III

THINKING LIKE A PORTFOLIO MANAGER

6

THE TOP-DOWN METHOD

So if you're bullish on Financials, how much of your portfolio should you put in Financials stocks? Twenty-five percent? Fifty? One hundred percent? This question concerns portfolio management. Most investors concern themselves only with individual companies ("I like Bank of America, so I'll buy some") without considering how they fit into their overall portfolio. But this is no way to manage your money.

In this part of the book, we show you how to analyze Financials companies like a top-down portfolio manager. This includes a full description of the top-down method, how to use benchmarks and how the top-down method applies to the Financials sector. We then explore security analysis in Chapter 7, where we provide a framework for analyzing any company and discuss many of the important questions to ask when analyzing Financials companies. Finally, in Chapter 8, we conclude by giving a few examples of specific investing strategies for the Financials sector.

INVESTING IS A SCIENCE

Too many investors today think investing has "rules"—that all one must do to succeed in investing for the long run is find the right set of investing rules. But that simply doesn't work. Why? All well-known and widely discussed information is already reflected in stock prices. This is a basic tenet of market theory commonly referred to as "market efficiency." So if you see a headline about a stock you follow, there's no use trading on that information—it's already priced in. You missed the move.

If everything known is already discounted in prices, the only way to consistently beat the market is to know something others don't. Think about it: There are many intelligent investors and long-time professionals who fail to beat the market year after year, most with the same access to information as anyone, if not more. Why?

Most view investing as a craft. They think, "If I learn the craft of value investing and all its rules, then I can be a successful investor using that method." But that simply can't work because by definition, all the conventional ways of thinking about value investing will already be widely known and thus priced in. In fact, most investment styles are very well-known and already widely practiced. There are undoubtedly millions of investors out there much like you, looking at the same metrics and information you are. So there isn't much power in them. Even the investing techniques themselves are widely known—taught to millions in universities and practiced by hundreds of thousands of professionals globally. There's no edge.

Moreover, it's been demonstrated investment styles move in and out of favor over time—no one style or category is inherently better than another in the long run. You may think "value" investing works wonders to beat markets, but the fact is growth stocks will trounce value at times.

The key to beating stock markets lies in being dynamic—never adhering for all time to a single investment idea—and gleaning information the market hasn't yet priced in. In other words, you cannot adhere to a single set of "rules" and hope to outperform markets over time.

So how can you beat the markets? By thinking of investing as a science.

Einstein's Brain and the Stock Market

If he weren't so busy becoming the most renowned scientist of the twentieth century, Albert Einstein would have made a killing on Wall

Street—but not because he had such a high IQ. Granted, he was immensely intelligent, but a high IQ alone does not make a market guru. (If it did, MIT professors would be making millions managing money instead of teaching.) Instead, it's the style of his thought and the method of his work that matter.

In the little we know about Einstein's investment track record, he didn't do very well. He lost most of his Nobel Prize money in bad bond ventures.[1] Heck, Sir Isaac Newton may have given us the three laws of motion, but even his talents didn't extend to investing. He lost his shirt in the South Sea Bubble of the early 1700s, explaining later, "I can calculate the movement of the stars, but not the madness of men."

So why believe Einstein would have been a great portfolio manager if he put his mind to it? In short, Einstein was a true and highly creative scientist. He didn't take the acknowledged rules of physics as such—he used prior knowledge, logic and creativity, combined with the rigors of verifiable, testable scientific method to create an entirely new view of the cosmos. In other words, he was dynamic and gleaned knowledge others didn't have. Investors should do the same. (Not to worry, you won't need advanced calculus to do it.)

Einstein's unique character gave him an edge—he truly had a mind made to beat markets. Scientists have studied his work, his speeches, his letters, even his brain (literally) to find the secret of his intellect. In all, his approach to information processing and idea generation, his willingness to go against the grain of the establishment and his relentless pursuit of answers to questions no one else was asking ultimately made him a genius.

Most biographers and his contemporaries agree one of Einstein's foremost gifts was his ability to discern "the big picture." Unlike many scientists who could easily drown themselves in data minutiae, Einstein had an ability to see above the fray. Another way to say this is he could take the same information everyone else at his time was looking at and interpret it differently, yet correctly. He accomplished this using his talent for extracting the most important data from what he studied and linking them together in innovative ways no one else could.

Einstein called this "combinatory play." Similar to a child experimenting with a new Lego set, Einstein would combine and recombine seemingly unrelated ideas, concepts and images to produce new, original discoveries. In the end, almost all new ideas are merely the combination of existing ones in one form or another. Take $E = mc^2$: Einstein was not the first to discover the concepts of energy, mass or the speed of light. Rather, he combined these concepts in a novel way and, in the process, altered the way in which we view the universe.[2]

Einstein's combinatory play is a terrific metaphor for stock investing. To be a successful market strategist, you must be able to extract the most important data from all of the "noise" permeating today's markets and generate conclusions the market hasn't yet appreciated. Central to this task is your ability to link data together in unique ways and produce new insights and themes for your portfolio in the process.

Einstein learned science basics just like his peers. But once he had those mastered, he directed his brain to challenging prior assumptions and inventing entirely different lenses to look through.

This is why this book isn't intended to give you a "silver bullet" for picking the right Financials stocks. The fact is the "right" Financials stocks will be different in different times and situations. You don't have to be Einstein, you just should think differently—and like a scientist—if you want to beat markets.

THE TOP-DOWN METHOD

Overwhelmingly, investment professionals today do what can broadly be labeled "bottom-up" investing. Their emphasis is on stock selection. A typical bottom-up investor researches an assortment of companies and attempts to pick those with the greatest likelihood of outperforming the market based on individual merits. The selected securities are cobbled together to form a portfolio, and factors like country and economic sector exposure are purely residuals of security selection, not planned decisions.

"Top-down" investing reverses the order. A top-down investor first analyzes big-picture factors like economics, politics and sentiment to forecast which investment categories are most likely to outperform the market. Only then does a top-down investor begin looking at individual securities. Top-down investing is inevitably more concerned with a portfolio's aggregate exposure to investment categories than with any individual security. Thus, top-down is an inherently dynamic mode of investment because investment strategies are based on the prevailing market and economic environment (which changes often).

There's significant debate in the investment community as to which approach is superior. This book's goal is not to reject bottom-up investing—there are indeed investors who've successfully utilized bottom-up approaches. Rather, the goal is to introduce a comprehensive and flexible methodology any investor could use to build a portfolio designed to beat the global stock market in any investment environment. It's a framework for gleaning new insights and making good on information not already reflected in stock prices.

Before we describe the method, let's explore several key reasons a top-down approach is advantageous:

- **Scalability:** A bottom-up process is akin to looking for needles in a haystack. A top-down process is akin to seeking the haystacks with the highest concentration of needles. Globally, there are nearly 25,000 publicly traded stocks. Even the largest institutions with the greatest research resources cannot hope to adequately examine all these companies. Smaller institutions and individual investors must prioritize where to focus their limited resources. Unlike a bottom-up process, a top-down process makes this gargantuan task manageable by determining, upfront, what slices of the market to examine at the security level.
- **Enhanced stock selection:** Well-designed top-down processes generate insights that can greatly enhance stock selection. Macroeconomic or political analysis, for instance, can help determine what types of strategic attributes will face headwinds or tailwinds (see Chapter 7 for a full explanation).

- **Risk control:** Bottom-up processes are highly subject to unintended risk concentrations. Top-down processes are inherently better suited to manage risk exposures throughout the investment process.
- **Macro overview:** Top-down processes are more conducive to avoiding macro-driven calamities like the bursting of the Japan bubble in the 1990s, the Technology bubble in 2000 or the 2000 to 2002 bear market. No matter how good an individual company may be, it is still beholden to sector, regional and broad market factors. In fact, there is evidence "macro" factors can largely determine a stock's performance regardless of individual merit.

Top-Down Means Thinking 70-20-10

A top-down investment process also helps focus on what's most important to investment results: asset allocation and sub-asset allocation decisions. Many investors focus most of their attention on security-level portfolio decisions, like picking individual stocks they think will perform well. However, studies have shown over 90% of return variability is derived from asset allocation decisions, not market timing or stock selection.[3]

Our research shows about 70% of return variability is derived from asset allocation, 20% from sub-asset allocation (such as country, sector, size and style) and 10% from security selection. While security selection can make a significant difference over time, higher-level portfolio decisions dominate investment results more often than not.

The balance of this chapter defines the various steps in the top-down method, specifically as they relate to making country, sector and style decisions. This same basic framework can be applied to portfolios to make allocations within sectors. At the end of the chapter, we detail how this framework can be applied to the Financials sector.

Benchmarks

A key part of the top-down model is using benchmarks. A benchmark is typically a broad-based index of securities such as the S&P

500, MSCI World or Russell 2000. Benchmarks are indispensable road maps for structuring a portfolio, monitoring risk and judging performance over time.

Tactically, a portfolio should be structured to maximize the probability of consistently beating the benchmark. This is inherently different from maximizing returns. Unlike aiming to achieve some fixed rate of return each year, which will cause disappointment relative to peers when capital markets are very strong and is potentially unrealistic when the capital markets are very weak, a properly benchmarked portfolio provides a realistic guide for dealing with uncertain market conditions.

Portfolio construction begins by evaluating the characteristics of the chosen benchmark: sector weights, country weights and market cap and valuations. Then an expected risk and return is assigned to each of these segments (based on portfolio drivers), and the most attractive areas are overweighted, while the least attractive are underweighted. Table 6.1 shows MSCI World benchmark sector characteristics as of December 31, 2011, as an example, Table 6.2 shows country characteristics and Table 6.3 shows market cap and valuations.

Based on benchmark characteristics, portfolio drivers are then used to determine country, sector and style decisions for the portfolio. For

Table 6.1   MSCI World Characteristics—Sectors

Sector	Total
Financials	17.6%
Information Technology	12.0%
Energy	11.8%
Industrials	11.0%
Consumer Staples	11.0%
Health Care	10.5%
Consumer Discretionary	10.3%
Materials	7.2%
Telecommunication Services	4.4%
Utilities	4.0%

Source: Thomson Reuters; MSCI, Inc.[4] MSCI World Index as of 12/31/11.

Table 6.2   MSCI World Characteristics—Countries

Country	Total
US	52.7%
UK	9.8%
Japan	9.1%
Canada	5.2%
France	3.8%
Switzerland	3.6%
Australia	3.6%
Germany	3.3%
Spain	1.4%
Sweden	1.3%
Hong Kong	1.2%
Netherlands	1.1%
Italy	1.0%
Singapore	0.7%
Denmark	0.4%
Belgium	0.4%
Norway	0.4%
Finland	0.4%
Israel	0.3%
Ireland	0.1%
Austria	0.1%
Portugal	0.1%
New Zealand	0.0%
Greece	0.0%

Source: Thomson Reuters; MSCI, Inc.,[5] MSCI World Index as of 12/31/11.

example, the Financials sector weight in the MSCI World Index is about 18%.[7] Therefore, a portfolio managed against this benchmark would consider an 18% weight in Financials "neutral," or market-weighted. If you believe Financials will perform better than the market in the foreseeable future, then you would "overweight" the sector, or carry a percentage of stocks in your portfolio greater than 18%. The reverse is true for an "underweight"—you'd hold less than 18% in Financials if you were pessimistic on the sector looking ahead.

Table 6.3   MSCI World Characteristics—Market Cap and Valuations

	Valuations
Weighted Average Market Cap (bil)	$68.5
Median Market Cap (bil)	$7,687
Median P/E	13.4
Median P/B	1.6
Median P/CF	7.8
Median P/S	1.2
Median Dividend Yield (%)	2.4
Number of Holdings	1,615

Notes: Market Cap in US Billions, P/E = price to earnings, P/B = price to book, P/CF = price to cash flow, P/S = price to sales.

Source: Thomson Reuters; MSCI, Inc.,[6] MSCI World Index as of 12/31/11.

Note that being pessimistic on Financials doesn't necessarily mean holding zero stocks. It might only mean holding a lesser percentage of stocks in your portfolio than the benchmark. This is an important feature of benchmarking—it allows an investor to make strategic decisions on sectors and countries but maintains diversification, thus managing risk more appropriately.

For the Financials sector, we can use Financials-specific benchmarks like the S&P 500 Financials, MSCI World Financials or Russell 2000 Financials indexes. The components of these benchmarks can then be evaluated at a more detailed level, such as industry and sub-industry weights. (For example, we broke out MSCI World industry and sub-industry benchmark weights in Chapter 1.)

TOP-DOWN DECONSTRUCTED

The top-down method begins by first analyzing the macro environment. It asks the "big" questions like: Do you think stocks will go up or down in the next 12 months? Which countries or sectors should benefit most? Once you have decided on these high-level portfolio "drivers" (sometimes called "themes"), you can examine various macro portfolio drivers to make general overweight and underweight decisions for countries, sectors, industries and sub-industries versus your benchmark.

For instance, let's say we've determined a macroeconomic driver that goes something like this: "In the next 12 months, I believe global economic growth will be slower than most expect." That's a very high-level statement with important implications for your portfolio. It means you'd want to search for stocks that would benefit most from weakening economic growth and activity.

The second step in top-down is applying quantitative screening criteria to narrow the choice set of stocks. Since, in our hypothetical example, we believe economic growth will be weak, we could take a neutral stance on Financials stocks and focus on more defensive industries within.

But which ones? Are you bullish on, say, Insurance Brokers? Government-focused office REITs? Fixed-income asset managers? Do you want exposure to the US or another region? Do you want small-cap Financials companies or large cap? And what about valuations? Are you looking for growth or value? (Size and growth versus value decisions are often referred to as "style" decisions.) These criteria and more can help you narrow the list of stocks you might buy.

The third and final step is performing fundamental analysis on individual stocks. Notice a great deal of thinking, analysis and work is done before you ever think about individual stocks. That's the key to the top-down approach: It emphasizes high-level themes and funnels its way down to individual stocks, as illustrated in Figure 6.1.

Step 1: Analyze Portfolio Drivers and Country and Sector Selection

Let's examine the first step in the top-down method more closely. In order to make top-down decisions, we develop and analyze what we call portfolio drivers (as mentioned previously). We segment these portfolio drivers in three general categories: economic, political and sentiment.

Portfolio drivers are what drive the performance of a broad category of stocks. Accurately identifying current and future drivers will

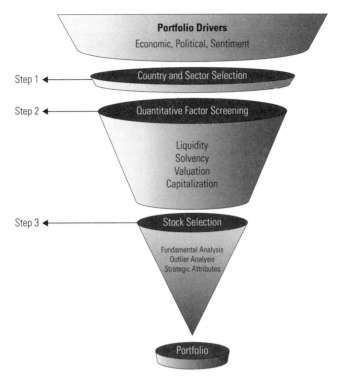

Figure 6.1   Top-Down Deconstructed

help you find areas of the market most likely to outperform or under-perform your benchmark (i.e., the broader stock market).

Table 6.4 shows examples of each type of portfolio driver. It's important to note these drivers are by no means comprehensive, nor are they valid for all time periods. In fact, correctly identifying new portfolio drivers is essential to beating the market in the long term.

Economic Drivers   Economic drivers are anything related to the macroeconomic environment. This could include monetary policy, interest rates, lending activity, yield curve analysis, relative GDP growth analysis and myriad others. What economic forces are likely to drive GDP growth throughout countries in the world? What is the outlook for interest rates, and how would that impact sectors? What is the outlook for loan growth or employment trends among countries?

Table 6.4   Portfolio Drivers

Economic	Political	Sentiment
Economic growth	Structural reform/liberalization	Fear versus greed
Interest rates	Energy & environmental policy	Growth versus value
Inflation	Nationalization/privatization	Mutual fund flows
Commodity prices	Regulatory environment	Media coverage
Capital investment	Taxation	Consumer confidence
Industrial production	Property rights	Risk aversion
Employment	Government stability	Momentum cycle analysis
Housing markets	Trade policy	Foreign investment
Exchange rates	Geopolitical conflict	Professional investor forecasts
Foreign trade		

Economic drivers pertain not only to the fundamental outlook of the economy (GDP growth, interest rates, inflation), but also to the stock market (valuations, M&A activity, share buybacks). As an investor, it's your job to identify these drivers and determine how they'll impact your overall portfolio and each of its segments.

The following is a sample list of economic drivers that could impact portfolio performance:

- US economic growth will be higher than consensus expectations.
- European Union interest rates will remain benign.
- Mergers, acquisitions and share buybacks will be strong.
- Emerging Markets growth will drive commodity demand.

Political Drivers   Political drivers can be country-specific, pertain to regions (European Union, Organisation for Economic Cooperation and Development [OECD]) or affect interaction between countries or regions (such as trade policies). These drivers are more concerned with categories such as taxation, government stability, fiscal policy and political turnover. Which countries are experiencing a change in government that could have a meaningful impact on their economies? Which sectors could be at risk from new taxation or legislation? Which countries are undergoing pro-growth reforms?

Political drivers will help determine the relative attractiveness of market segments and countries based on the outlook for the political environment. Be warned, however: Most investors suffer from "home country bias," where they ascribe too much emphasis to the politics of their own country. Always keep in mind it's a big, interconnected world out there, and geopolitical developments everywhere can have implications.

What are possible political drivers you can find? The following is a list of examples that can drive stocks up or down:

- Political party change in Japan driving pro-growth reforms.
- New tax policies in Germany stalling economic growth.
- Protests, government coups and conflict driving political instability in Thailand.

Sentiment Drivers Sentiment drivers attempt to measure consensus thinking about investment categories. Ideally, drivers identify market opportunities where sentiment is different from reality. For example, let's say you observe current broad market sentiment expects a US recession in the next year. But you disagree and believe GDP growth will be strong. This presents an excellent opportunity for excess returns. You can load up on stocks that will benefit from an economic boom and watch the prices rise as the rest of the market realizes it much later.

Since the market is a discounter of all known information, it's important to try to identify what the market is pricing in. The interpretation of such investor drivers is typically counterintuitive (avoid what is overly popular and seek what is largely unpopular). Looking forward, which sectors are investors most bullish about and why? What countries or sectors are widely discussed in the media? What market segments have been bid up recently based on something other than fundamentals? If the market's perception is different from fundamentals in the short term, stocks will eventually correct themselves to reflect reality in the long term.

A note of caution: Gauging market sentiment does not mean being a contrarian. Contrarians are investors who simply do the opposite of what most believe will happen. Instead, find places where sentiment (people's beliefs) doesn't match what you believe is reality and over- or underweight sections of your portfolio accordingly, relative to your benchmark. Examples of sentiment drivers include:

- Investors remain pessimistic about Financials despite improving fundamentals.
- Sentiment for the Chinese stock market approaching euphoria, stretching valuations.
- Professional investors universally forecast US small-cap stocks will outperform.

How to Create Your Own Investment Drivers

In order to form your own investment drivers, the first step is accessing a wide array of data from multiple sources. For country drivers, this could range from globally focused publications like *The Wall Street Journal* or *Financial Times* to regional newspapers or government data. For sector drivers, this could include reading trade publications or following major company announcements.

Remember, however, markets are efficient—they reflect all widely known information. Most pertinent information about public companies is, well, public. Which means the market already knows. News travels fast, and investors with the knowledge and expectations are absorbed by markets very quickly. Those seeking to profit on a bit of news, rumor or speculation must acknowledge the market will probably move faster than they can. Therefore, in order to consistently generate excess returns, you must either know something others don't or interpret widely known information correctly and differently from the crowd. (For a detailed discussion of these factors and more, read *The Only Three Questions That Still Count* by Ken Fisher.)

Step 2: Quantitative Factor Screening

Step two in the top-down method is screening for quantitative factors. This allows you to narrow the potential list of stocks once your portfolio drivers are in place.

There are thousands and thousands of stocks out there, so it's vital to use a series of factors like market capitalization and valuations to narrow the field a bit. Securities passing this screen are then subjected to further quantitative analysis that eliminates companies with excessive risk profiles relative to their peer group, such as companies with excessive leverage or balance sheet risk and securities lacking sufficient liquidity for investment.

The rigidity of the quantitative screens is entirely up to you and will determine the number of companies on your prospect list. The more rigid the criteria, the fewer the companies that make the list. Broader criteria will increase the number of companies.

Examples   How can you perform such a screen? Here are two examples of quantitative factor screenings to show how broad or specific you can be. You might want to apply very strict criteria, or you may prefer to be broader.

Strict Criteria

- First, you decide you want to search for only Financials firms. By definition, that excludes all companies from the other nine sectors. Already, you've narrowed the field a lot!
- Now, let's say based on your high-level drivers, you only want European Financials stocks. By excluding all other regions besides Europe, you've narrowed the field even more.
- Next, let's decide to search only for Diversified Financials firms in the Financials sector.
- Perhaps you don't believe very small stocks are preferable, so you limit market capitalization to $3 billion and above.
- Last, let's set some parameters for valuation:
  - P/E (price to earnings) less than 14x
  - P/B (price to book) less than 2x
  - P/CF (price to cash-flow) less than 10x
  - P/S (price to sales) less than 3x

This rigorous process of selecting parameters will yield a small number of stocks to research, all based on your higher-level themes.

But maybe you have reason to be less specific and want to do a broader screen because you think Financials in general is a good place to be. A broad screen might have only the following criteria:

- Financials sector
- Global (no country or region restrictions)
- Market caps above $1 billion

This selection process is much broader and obviously gives you a much longer list of stocks to choose from. Neither a strict nor broad screen is inherently better. It just depends on how well-formed and specific your higher-level themes are. Obviously, a stricter screen means less work for you in step three—actual stock selection.

Step 3: Stock Selection

After narrowing the prospect list, your final step is identifying individual securities possessing strategic attributes consistent with higher-level portfolio themes. (We'll cover the stock selection process specifically in more detail in Chapter 8.) Your stock selection process should attempt to accomplish two goals:

1. Seek firms possessing strategic attributes consistent with higher-level portfolio themes, derived from the drivers that give those firms a competitive advantage versus their peers. For example, if you believe owning firms with dominant market shares in consolidating industries is a favorable characteristic, you would search for firms with that profile.

2. Seek to maximize the likelihood of beating the category of stocks you are analyzing. For example, if you want a certain portfolio weight of REITs and need 4 stocks out of 12 meeting the quantitative criteria, you then pick the 4 that, as a group, maximize the likelihood of beating all 12 as a whole. This is different from trying to pick "the best four." By avoiding stocks likely to be extreme or "weird" outliers versus the

group, you can reduce portfolio risk while adding value at the security selection level.

In lieu of picking individual securities, there are other ways to exploit high-level themes in the top-down process. For instance, if you feel strongly about a particular sub-industry but don't think you can add value through individual security analysis, it may be more prudent to buy a group of companies in the sub-industry or a category product like an exchange-traded fund (ETF). There is a growing variety of ETFs that track the domestic and global Financials sector and industries. This way, you can be sure to gain broad Financials exposure without much stock-specific risk. (For more information on ETFs, visit www.ishares.com, www.sectorspdr.com or www.master-data.com.)

MANAGING AGAINST A FINANCIALS BENCHMARK

Now we can practice translating this specifically to your Financials allocation. Just as you analyze the components of your benchmark to determine country and sector components in a top-down strategy, you must analyze each sector's components, as we did in Chapters 2–5. To demonstrate how, we'll use the MSCI World Financials Sector Index as the benchmark. Table 6.5 shows the MSCI World Financials sub-industry weights as of December 31, 2011. We don't know what the sample portfolio weights should be, but we know it should add up to 100%. Of course, if managing against a broader benchmark, your Financials sector weight may add up to more or less than the Financials weight in the benchmark, depending on over- or underweight decisions.

Keeping the sub-industry weights in mind will help mitigate benchmark risk. If you have a portfolio of stocks with the same sub-industry weights as the MSCI World Financials Index, you're neutral—taking no benchmark risk. However, if you feel strongly about a sub-industry, like Insurance Brokers, and decide to purchase only those firms (one of the smallest weights in the sector),

Table 6.5   MSCI World Financials Sub-Industry Weights Versus Sample Portfolio

Industry	MSCI World (%)	Sample Portfolio
Banks	41%	?
Diversified Financials	23%	?
Insurance	21%	?
Real Estate	15%	?
Total	**100%**	**100%**

Source: Thomson Reuters; MSCI, Inc.,[8] MSCI World Index as of 12/31/11.

Table 6.6   Portfolio A

Industry	MSCI World (%)	Sample Portfolio	Difference
Banks	41%	50%	9%
Diversified Financials	23%	21%	−2%
Insurance	21%	16%	−5%
Real Estate	15%	13%	−2%
Total	**100%**	**100%**	**0%**

Source: Thomson Reuters; MSCI, Inc.,[9] MSCI World Index as of 12/31/11.

you're taking huge benchmark risk. The same is true if you significantly underweight a sub-industry. All the same rules apply as when you do this from a broader portfolio perspective, as we did earlier in this chapter.

The benchmark's sub-industry weights provide a jumping-off point in making further portfolio decisions. Once you make higher-level decisions on the sub-industries, you can make choices versus the benchmark by overweighting the sub-industries you feel likeliest to perform best and underweighting those likeliest to perform worst. Table 6.6 shows how you can make different portfolio bets against the benchmark by over- and underweighting sub-industries. *Note: Portfolio A might be a portfolio of all Financials stocks, or it can simply represent a neutral Financials sector allocation in a larger portfolio.*

Table 6.7   Portfolio B

Industry	MSCI World (%)	Sample Portfolio	Difference
Banks	41%	70%	29%
Diversified Financials	23%	5%	−18%
Insurance	21%	12%	−9%
Real Estate	15%	13%	−2%
Total	**100%**	**100%**	0%

Source: Thomson Reuters; MSCI, Inc.,[10] MSCI World Index as of 12/31/11.

The "difference" column shows the relative difference between the benchmark and Portfolio A. In this example, Portfolio A is most over-weight to Banks and most underweight to Insurance.

In other words, for this hypothetical example, Portfolio A's owner expects Banks to outperform the sector and Insurance to underperform the sector. But in terms of benchmark risk, Portfolio A remains fairly close to the benchmark weights, so its relative risk is quite modest. This is extremely important: By managing against a benchmark, you can make strategic choices to beat the index and are well-diversified within the sector without concentrating too heavily in a specific area.

Table 6.7 is another example of relative portfolio weighting versus the benchmark. Portfolio B is significantly underweight to Diversified Financials with exposure concentrated in Banks. Because the sub-industry weights are so different from the benchmark, Portfolio B takes on substantially more relative risk than Portfolio A.

Regardless of how your portfolio is positioned relative to the benchmark, it's important to use benchmarks to identify where your relative risks are before investing. Knowing the benchmark weights and having opinions on the future performance of each sub-industry is a crucial step in building a portfolio designed to beat the bench-mark. Should you make the correct overweight and underweight deci-sions, you're likelier to beat the benchmark, regardless of the individual securities held within. But even if you're wrong, you'll have diversified enough not to lose your shirt.

Top-Down Recap

A more effective approach to sector analysis is "top-down." A top-down investment methodology analyzes big-picture factors such as economics, politics and sentiment to forecast which investment categories are likely to outperform the market. A key part of the process is using benchmarks (such as the MSCI World Financials or S&P 500 Financials indexes), which are used as guidelines for building portfolios, monitoring performance and managing risk. By analyzing portfolio drivers, we can identify which Financials industries and sub-industries are most attractive and unattractive, ultimately filtering down to stock selection.

- The top-down investment methodology first identifies and analyzes high-level portfolio drivers affecting broad categories of stocks. These drivers help determine portfolio country, sector and style weights. The same methodology can be applied to a specific sector to determine industry and sub-industry weights.

- Quantitative factor screening helps narrow the list of potential portfolio holdings based on characteristics such as valuations, liquidity and solvency.

- Stock selection is the last step in the top-down process. Stock selection attempts to find companies possessing strategic attributes consistent with higher-level portfolio drivers.

- Stock selection also attempts to find companies with the greatest probability of outperforming their peers.

- It's helpful to use a Financials benchmark as a guide when constructing a portfolio to determine your sub-industry overweights and underweights.

7

SECURITY ANALYSIS

Now that we've covered the top-down method, let's pick some stocks. This chapter walks you through analyzing individual Financials firms using the top-down method presented in Chapter 6. Specifically, we'll demonstrate a five-step process for analyzing firms relative to peers.

Every firm and every stock is different, and viewing them through the right lens is vital. Investors need a functional, consistent and reusable framework for analyzing securities across the sector. While by no means comprehensive, the framework provided and the questions at this chapter's end should serve as good starting points to help identify strategic attributes and company-specific risks.

While volumes have been written about individual security analysis, a top-down investment approach de-emphasizes the importance of stock selection in a portfolio. As such, we'll talk about the basics of stock analysis for the beginner-to-intermediate investor. For a more thorough understanding of financial statement analysis, valuations, modeling and other tools of security analysis, additional reading is suggested.

Top-Down Recap

As covered in Chapter 6, you can use the top-down method to make your biggest, most important portfolio decisions first. However, the same process applies when picking stocks, and those high-level portfolio decisions ultimately filter down to individual securities.

Step one is analyzing the broader global economy and identifying various macro "drivers" affecting entire sectors or industries. Using the drivers, you can make general allocation decisions for countries, sectors, industries and sub-industries versus the given benchmark. Step two is applying quantitative screening criteria to narrow the choice set of stocks. It's not until all those decisions are made that we get to analyze individual stocks. Security analysis is the third and final step.

For the rest of the chapter, we assume you have already established a benchmark, solidified portfolio themes, made sub-industry overweight and underweight decisions and are ready to analyze firms within a peer group. (A peer group is a group of stocks you'd generally expect to perform similarly because they operate in the same industry, possibly share the same geography and have similar quantitative attributes.)

MAKE YOUR SELECTION

Security analysis is nowhere near as complicated as it may seem—but that doesn't mean it's easy. Similar to your goal in choosing industry and sector weights, you've got one basic task: spotting opportunities not currently discounted into prices. Or, put differently, knowing something others don't. Investors should analyze a firm by taking consensus expectations for a company's estimated financial results and then assessing whether it will perform below, in line with or above those baseline expectations. Profit opportunities arise when your expectations are different and more accurate than consensus expectations. Trading on widely known information or consensus expectations adds no value to the stock selection process. Doing so is really no different than trading on a coin flip.

The top-down method offers two ways to spot such opportunities. First, accurately predict high-level, macro themes affecting an industry or group of companies—these are your portfolio drivers. Second, find firms that will benefit most if those high-level themes and drivers play out. This is done by finding firms with competitive advantages (we'll explain this concept more in a bit).

Since the majority of excess return is added in higher-level decisions in the top-down process, it's not vital to pick the "best" stocks in the universe. Rather, you want to pick stocks with a good probability of outperforming their peers. Doing so can enhance returns without jeopardizing good top-down decisions by picking risky, go-big-or-go-home stocks. Being right more often than not should create outperformance relative to the benchmark over time.

A FIVE-STEP PROCESS

Analyzing a stock against its peer group can be summarized as a five-step process:

1. Understand business and earnings drivers.
2. Identify strategic attributes.
3. Analyze fundamental and stock price performance.
4. Identify risks.
5. Analyze valuations and consensus expectations.

These five steps provide a consistent framework for analyzing firms in their peer groups. While these steps are far from a full stock analysis, they provide the basics necessary to begin making better stock selections.

Step 1: Understand Business and Earnings Drivers

The first step is understanding what the business does, how it generates its earnings and what drives those earnings. Here are a few tips to help in the process.

- **Industry overview:** Begin any analysis with a basic understanding of the firm's industry, including its drivers and risks. You should be familiar with how current economic trends affect the industry.
- **Company description:** Obtain a business description of the company, including descriptions of the products and services within each business segment. It's always best to go directly to a company's financial statements for this. (Almost every public firm makes its financial statements readily accessible online these days.) Browse the firm's Website and financial statements/reports to gain an overview of the company and how it presents itself.
- **Corporate history:** Read the firm's history since its inception and over the last several years. An understanding of firm history may reveal its growth strategy or consistency with success and failure. It also will provide clues on what its true core competencies are. Ask questions like: Has it been an industry leader for decades, or is it a relative newcomer? Has it switched strategies or businesses often in the past?
- **Business segments:** Break down company revenues and earnings by business segment and geography to determine how and where it makes its money. Find out what drives results in each business and geographic segment. Begin thinking about how each of these business segments fits into your high-level themes.
- **Recent news/press releases:** Read all recently released news about the stock, including press releases. Do a Google search and see what comes up. Look for any significant announcements regarding company operations. What is the media's opinion of the firm? Is it a bellwether to the industry or a minor player?
- **Markets and customers:** Identify main customers and the markets it operates in. Determine whether the firm has any particularly large single customer or a concentrated customer base.

- **Competition:** Find the main competitors and how their market share compares with other industry players. Is the industry highly segmented? Assess the industry's competitive landscape. Keep in mind the biggest competitors can sometimes lurk in different industries—sometimes even in different sectors! Get a feel for how the firm stacks up—is it an industry leader or a minor player? Does market share matter in that industry?

Step 2: Identify Strategic Attributes

After gaining a solid grasp of firm operations, the next step is identifying strategic attributes consistent with higher-level portfolio themes. Also known as competitive or comparative advantages, strategic attributes are unique features allowing firms to outperform their industry or sector. Since industry peers are generally affected by the same high-level drivers, strong strategic attributes are the edge in creating superior performance. Examples of strategic attributes include:

- Favorable regulatory regime
- High relative market share
- Low-cost production
- Superior sales relationships/distribution
- Economic sensitivity
- Vertical integration
- Strong management/business strategy
- Geographic diversity or advantage
- Consolidator
- Strong balance sheet
- Niche market exposure
- Pure play
- Potential takeover target
- Proprietary technologies
- Strong brand name
- First mover advantage

Strategic Attributes: Making Lemonade

How do strategic attributes help you analyze individual stocks? Consider a simple example: There are five lemonade stands of similar size, product and quality within a city block. A scorching heat wave envelops the city, sending a rush of customers in search of lemonade. Which stand benefits most from the industry-wide surge in business? This likely depends on each stand's strategic attributes. Maybe one is a cost leader and has the cheapest access to homegrown lemons. Maybe one has a geographic advantage and is located next to a basketball court full of thirsty players. Or maybe one has a superior business strategy with a "buy two, get one free" initiative that drives higher sales volume and a bigger customer base. Any of these are core strategic advantages.

Portfolio drivers help determine which kind of strategic attributes are likely to face headwinds or tailwinds. After all, not all strategic attributes will benefit a firm in all environments. For example, while higher operating leverage might help a firm boost earnings in the booming part of an industry, it would have the opposite effect in a down cycle.

A pertinent example in the Financials sector is an asset manager focused on equity investments. During periods of rising equity prices, the company's exposure to equities will allow its assets under management (AUM) to increase naturally and drive higher revenue. However, when equity prices fall, this exposure can quickly erode its AUM. Thus, it's essential to pick strategic attributes consistent with higher-level portfolio themes and analyze those that are more important in the current environment.

A strategic attribute is also only effective to the extent management recognizes and takes advantage of it. Execution is key. For example, a bank may be strategically positioned in a geographic region with demand growth, but it can capitalize on this advantage only if it has sufficient capital to support a growing balance sheet.

Identifying strategic attributes may require thorough research of the firm's financial statements, Website, news stories and history and discussions with customers, suppliers, competitors or management. Don't skimp on this step—be diligent and thorough in finding strategic attributes. It may feel like an arduous task at times, but it's also among the most important in security selection.

Step 3: Analyze Fundamental and Stock Price Performance

Once you've gained a thorough understanding of the business, earnings drivers and strategic attributes, the next step is analyzing firm performance both fundamentally and in the stock market. Using the latest earnings releases, annual reports and the company's conference calls with financial analysts, first analyze the company's recent financial performance. Ask the following questions:

- What are recent trends for revenues, margins and earnings? What business activities are driving results and how?
- Have earnings tended to be above or below company guidance? How did earnings compare to consensus estimates?
- Are earnings growing because of higher volumes, higher prices or lower costs?
- Are headline earnings affected by one-off accounting items?
- Were there any major regulatory events? How might they impact future financial performance?
- Is the company growing organically, because of acquisitions or for some other reason?
- Is the company generating sufficient operating cash flow to fund its capital investments? If not, how is it financing the difference? Can the company obtain capital at attractive rates?
- What is management's strategy for the future? Will management invest in growth or return excess capital to shareholders?
- How sustainable is the strategy? Is it predicated on realistic macroeconomic assumptions?
- What is the financial health of the company? Does it have sufficient liquidity to meet its financial obligations?

After familiarizing yourself with the company, evaluate some of its peers. You'll begin to notice similar trends and events affecting the broader industry. Take note of these so you can distinguish between issues that are company specific or industry wide.

Once you've got a sense of the company's fundamental financial performance, check the company's stock chart for the last few years. In light of the financial statements you've reviewed, does the stock chart look like you would expect?

Explain any big up or down moves in the company's share price, and identify any significant news events. If the stock price has trended steadily downward despite ostensibly strong financial performance, the market may be discounting an expected future event—perhaps the market is expecting a drop in housing prices will elevate future loan losses.

Or if the company's share price has soared despite weak financial performance, there may be some unseen force driving shares higher, such as speculation the company may be a takeover target. Sometimes, stock-specific financial performance may be overshadowed by broad industry trends, such as rising interest rates or changes in regulation. Or stocks can simply move in sympathy with the broader market. Whatever it is, make sure you know.

Step 4: Identify Risks

There are two main types of risks in security analysis: stock-specific risk and systematic risk (also known as non-stock specific risk). Both can be equally important to performance.

Stock-specific risks, as the name suggests, are issues affecting the company in isolation. These are mainly risks affecting a firm's business operations or future operations. Some company-specific risks are discussed in detail in the 10-K for US firms and the 20-F for foreign filers (found at www.sec.gov). But one can't rely solely on firms self-identifying risk factors. You must see what analysts are saying about them and identify all risks for yourself. Some examples include:

- Regulatory proceedings
- High earnings sensitivity to commodity prices

- Customer concentration
- Supply chain risks
- Excessive leverage or lack of access to financing
- Poor operational track record
- High cost relative to competitors
- Late SEC filings
- Qualified audit opinions
- Hedging or trading activities
- Pension or benefit underfunding risk
- Outstanding litigation
- Pending corporate actions
- Executive departures
- Stock ownership concentration (insider or institutional)

Systematic risks include macroeconomic or geopolitical events out of a company's control. While the risks may affect a broad set of firms, they will have varying effects on each. Some examples include:

- Economic activity
- Commodity prices
- Interest rates
- Industry cost inflation
- Supply chain disruptions
- Legislative risk
- Geopolitical risks
- Weather

Identifying stock-specific risks helps an investor evaluate the relative risk and reward potential of firms within a peer group. Identifying systematic risks helps you make informed decisions about which sub-industries and countries to overweight or underweight.

If you don't feel strongly about any company in a peer group within a sub-industry you wish to overweight, you could pick the company with the least stock-specific risk. This would help achieve the goal of picking firms with the greatest probability of outperforming their peer group and still performing in line with your higher-level themes and drivers.

Step 5: Analyze Valuations and Consensus Expectations

Valuations can be tricky things. They are tools used to evaluate market sentiment and expectations for firms. They are not a foolproof way to see if a stock is "cheap" or "expensive." For example, most Financials firms have lower price to earnings than most information technology companies, but that doesn't necessarily make the sector a better value—IT companies earn their premium valuations by providing higher returns on capital and growth rates.

Investors are usually best served by comparing a firm's valuation to that of its peer group or relative to its own historical average. There are many different valuation metrics investors use in security analysis. Most look at the company's current share price relative to some financial metric—based on either historical performance or future expectations. Some of the most popular include:

- P/E—price to earnings
- P/B—price to book
- P/S—price to sales
- P/CF—price to cash flow
- DY—dividend yield
- EV/EBITDA—enterprise value to earnings before interest, taxes, depreciation and amortization

Even within a peer group, relative valuations in and of themselves do not provide insight into future stock performance. Just because one company's P/E is 20 while another's is 10 doesn't mean you should necessarily buy the one at 10 because it's "cheaper." When valuations are different, there's usually a reason, such as different strategic attributes, growth and profitability expectations and/or stock-specific risks. The main question for investors is thus, "Are valuations justified by fundamentals?" To answer this question, compile the valuations for a peer group and try to estimate why there are relative differences in valuation. Often, there's a strong relationship between valuations and financial performance.

However, valuations are not determined solely by a single financial metric. There are other, more qualitative factors that may provide a company with a higher—or lower—valuation than its financial performance might imply. For example, if an insurance company is in the midst of a contentious proceeding with its regulator, investors may assign a lower valuation multiple than its financial performance might otherwise imply. Or perhaps investors speculate an investment bank is a viable takeover target and provide a higher premium.

Once you understand the reasons for a financial company's relative valuation, you can then attempt to determine whether it's justified. For example, perhaps you find a company that has a low valuation because of an expected dividend cut. If your analysis leads you to believe analysts' earnings expectations are too conservative, you might conclude the company's dividend will be higher than expected, and thus the company's valuation multiple will expand.

Ultimately, valuations tell you what other investors think about a company's current and future prospects. Because stocks trade on the unexpected, understanding what investors expect is critical because it allows you to determine whether you believe reality will turn out to be better or worse than expected.

FINANCIALS ANALYSIS

While this chapter's framework can be used to analyze any firm, additional factors specific to the Financials sector must be considered. The following section provides some of the most important factors and questions to consider when researching firms in the sector. Answers to these questions should help distinguish between firms within a peer group and help identify strategic attributes and stock-specific risks. While there are countless other questions and factors that could and should be asked when researching Financials firms, these should serve as a good starting point.

Leverage ratios: Regulatory and non-regulatory leverage ratios can give a snapshot of a company's health. Many times, a company can have sufficient capital according to regulators, but this does not always match ratios the market demands. How much regulatory capital does the company have? What about other leverage ratios, such as the tangible equity ratio or leverage ratio?

Liquidity: Since the Financials sector is the most leveraged sector, it is highly reliant on credit markets for funding. How does the company fund its operations? Which sources of liquidity does the company tap? What is the company's loan-to-deposit ratio?

Exposures: Again due to the relatively high degree of leverage, it is important to properly scale a company's exposure to risk. What are the company's exposures relative to the company's equity? Is it taking too big of a bet?

Asset liability sensitivity: How will the company's balance sheet react to rising or falling interest rates? What about the income statement?

Product mix: It is important to know if a company is levered to products in a growing or shrinking category. Which types of loans does the company offer? What is the mix between consumer lending and business lending? Are the loans collateralized? Is the company exposed to fixed-income management or equity management?

Earnings variability: Financial companies are known for recurring "one-time gains and losses," but what do core earnings look like? How are core operations trending?

Sales growth: Net sales growth is a positive sign for a business, but as a stock analyst, you must determine how top-line sales growth is derived if you are to determine the quality of the sales growth. Was the top line influenced primarily by acquisitions or divestitures, or was it organic growth from ongoing operations? You can extrapolate organic growth into the future with more confidence than you can acquisition-based growth, so it is generally considered a more relevant analytic.

Geographic diversity: How wide is the firm's geographic reach? Does the firm have meaningful exposure to high-growth international markets? Is the firm concentrated in a slow-growth, mature market? Geographic diversification can help smooth earnings trends as growth in one market can offset weakness in other markets. If a company is expanding internationally, what are the region's penetration rates, and what do margins look like in those markets? For internationally diversified firms, keep in mind fluctuations in foreign currency values influence the way sales and earnings are reported in US dollars.

Competition and barriers to entry: What does the competitive landscape look like? Are there firmly entrenched market share leaders who are insulated from smaller competitors via high barriers to entry? Are there substitutes for the company's products or services?

Margins: Are margins growing or shrinking, and what is driving this movement? Has the company historically offset higher costs with higher prices? How do its margins compare to those of peers?

Business strategy: Has the company recently been acquiring or divesting businesses? If so, what are the drivers behind such activity? If the company is a consolidator, does it have a successful track record of creating positive synergies like increased operating leverage, capacity utilization and distribution network efficiencies? If a firm is in divestment mode, what were the catalysts, and what is the strategy looking forward? Is it moving into higher growth categories?

Management: What is management's reputation? Is a seasoned team with a strong track record of building the business and adding shareholder value in place? Has it executed on stated goals and met guidance to the Street? Has there been management turnover?

Brand equity: Is the brand highly recognizable and respected? What are the firm's strategies in promoting the brand? A well-respected brand gives a firm the ability to price its product above the competition and to more easily expand into new geographic regions.

Political risk: Financials and politics are closely tied together, and legislative changes can happen on a relatively frequent basis. Does the firm currently operate in a favorable regulatory environment? How does it compare to other geographic regions? How might regulation change?

Financial strength: Does the company have enough cash and cash flows to operate well into the future? Compare the firm's interest costs with the amount of operating income the business generates (interest coverage ratio). Will the firm require additional funds in the future to expand its operation? If so, is there capacity to take on more debt, or would the firm have to engage in an equity offering that may dilute existing shareholders? You can investigate financial health by comparing balance sheet financial ratios to peers'. Ratios such as long-term debt to capital and the current ratio can be used to assess a firm's capitalization structure and liquidity level. Comparing credit ratings to peers is another tool at your disposal. The primary credit agencies are Standard & Poor's, Moody's and Fitch.

Recall debt isn't necessarily a bad thing when defining financial strength—many firms generate an excellent return on borrowed funds. Understanding the capital structure of a firm and its history of generating returns on capital will help you appraise the optimal level of debt.

Dividend yield: Confidence in the sustainability of a company's cash flow and dividends is crucial. How stable do they appear? What's the company's payout ratio (dividend/net income)? Although there's no rule, if it's less than 0.7, it's probably less likely to be cut than a peer with a higher ratio.

Reinvestments: If a company's payout ratio is low, it may mean the company is investing a higher percentage of profits into future growth. Often, earnings growth is fueled by capital expenditures (capex) to increase coverage and capacity. How much of sales are capex? How efficient does the company's spending appear to be? What's the capex efficiency ratio (EBITDA/capex)? How do these ratios compare to peers'?

Create Your Own Metric   We have covered common industry factors, but with a little creativity, you can come up with your own. For example, if you're interested in finding stocks with a high dividend yield that aren't too volatile, create a yield/beta ratio. Finding companies with the higher yields per unit of beta may be an easy way to compare companies and identify a superior investment.

8

FINANCIALS INVESTING STRATEGIES

This chapter covers various investment strategies specifically for a Financials allocation, building on the knowledge in this book. The strategies include:

1. Adding value at the sector level
2. Adding value at the country or industry level
3. Adding value at the security level

While the strategies presented here are by no means comprehensive, they'll provide a good starting point for constructing a portfolio that can increase your likelihood of outperforming a benchmark. They should also spur some investment strategy ideas of your own. After all, using this framework to discover information few others have discovered yet is what investing is all about.

Also, though these strategies focus solely on Financials, they are meant to be used as part of an overarching strategy for a portfolio managed against a broader benchmark. Some investors may choose to manage a portfolio only of Financials stocks (or any other single sector). But in our view, for individual investors, managing against a broader benchmark increases both risk management and outperformance opportunities.

ADDING VALUE AT THE SECTOR LEVEL

Consistent with the top-down method, investors must first determine when it is appropriate to overweight or underweight the Financials sector relative to a broader portfolio benchmark. Some major factors contributing to this decision, covered in depth in Chapter 1, are shown in Table 8.1. Each driver should be considered not on its own, but in combination with other relevant drivers and also larger macroeconomic conditions. Also, don't take this table to mean overweight decisions can be driven by the mere number of positive drivers (and the same is true in reverse with underweight decisions). There can be, at any one time, many more meaningful drivers than we have space to list here. And some drivers are just more important than others. Most important, macroeconomic drivers can swamp sector, industry and sub-industry drivers.

Implementing Sector Overweights and Underweights

After the decision is made to overweight or underweight the sector, it's time to implement it. The first step is determining the sector weight relative to your benchmark. The relative bet size should be proportional

Table 8.1   When to Overweight and Underweight the Financials Sector

Driver/Factor	Bullish	Bearish
Economic growth	Mixed	Mixed
Interest rates	Stable	Volatile
Regulatory environment	Certain	Uncertain
Risk aversion	Falling	Rising
Style leadership	Value	Growth
Size leadership	Mixed	Mixed

to your conviction. Mild conviction should translate to a more modest bet against the benchmark. The stronger your conviction, the bigger your bet can be—within reason. A vital rule is to never make a bet so large that if you're wrong you inflict irreparable damage on your portfolio's return versus the benchmark.

Next comes determining the actual investments. One method is directly mimicking the sector by buying all the sector's stocks in direct proportion to your under- or overweight. Obviously, this can be time consuming and costly—particularly for individual investors working with relatively smaller pools of money—depending on the number of stocks. An easier and probably cheaper method of mimicking the sector composition is buying exchange-traded funds (ETF) or mutual funds. The following are some larger Financials ETFs and their stock tickers (again, this list is by no means exhaustive):

- Financial Select Sector SPDR (XLF)
- iShares S&P Global Financials Sector Index Fund (IXG)
- SPDR KBW Bank ETF (KBE)
- SPDR KBW Regional Bank ETF (KRE)
- iShares DJ US Financial Sector (IYF)
- Market Vectors Bank and Brokerage ETF (RKH)
- iShares US Broker Dealers (IAI)
- EGShares Financials GEMS ETF (EFN)
- Vanguard Financials ETF (VFH)

ADDING VALUE AT THE COUNTRY OR INDUSTRY LEVEL

A more advanced strategy is making country- and industry-level bets based on your top-down analysis. Each Financials industry and region falls in and out of favor periodically—no one area outperforms consistently over the long term. Your job is determining how pronounced the degree of leading or lagging will be, when it's likeliest to happen and whether it's likely to be profitable enough to make a bet.

Chapters 2–5 should provide a structure for asking relevant questions to assist such decisions. For example, Chapter 2 outlines key variables for identifying trends in regional and diversified banking firms, such as:

- What countries, regions and industries have the best prospects based on financial product penetration rates and spending patterns?
- What will drive regional and diversified bank performance? Loan growth, delinquency trends or both?
- What is the most popular loan category driving demand for credit? Auto? Corporate? Small and medium business? Is that likely to continue?

Once such questions are answered, they should be scrutinized by examining appropriate challenges and opportunities. Ultimately, your decision to overweight or underweight an industry relative to the benchmark should jibe with your high-level portfolio drivers. Note: *Always remember past performance is no guarantee of future performance.* No set of rules works for all time, and you should always analyze the entire situation before investing. The past is about understanding context and precedent for investing—it's not a road map for the future.

ADDING VALUE AT THE SECURITY LEVEL

A still more advanced strategy entails investing directly in individual firms. This strategy should be based on your sector, country and industry opinions and was covered in more depth in Chapters 2–5. Never forget, individual stock selection should be driven by higher-level, top-down portfolio themes. For example, if you have a strong conviction that, relative to expectations, loan growth is going to decelerate and credit quality will worsen, you know that is typically a period when Financials stocks tend to underperform (though not

Table 8.2   Examples of Top-Down Security Selection

Hypothesis	Area of Focus	Possible Candidates
US mortgage delinquency trends will improve.	US banks with large mortgage portfolios	Wells Fargo (WFC) Bank of America (BAC)
Increasing wealth in the EM should fuel consumer spending.	Regions, like Brazil and India, with relatively strong economic growth and low financial product penetration rates	Banco Bradesco (BBD) ICICI Bank (IBN)
M&A activity will be more robust than expected.	Investment banks focused on advisory businesses	Lazard Ltd (LAZ) Greenhill & Co (GHL)

always). And if the sector overall underperforms, even the best stock picking in the world means your Financials picks likely lag better-performing sector stocks.

However, in a period when Financials underperforms, if your stock pick does well, your overall sector allocation may perform as well or better than your sector benchmark—which can help your overall *relative* performance. And certainly, during periods when Financials does perform better than the overall market, if you can add value at the security level, you can improve your portfolio performance on both an absolute and a relative basis.

In Table 8.2, we provide some examples of strategies for top-down security selection—though there are countless others. Further, the stocks named are just a few of those that, as of this writing, are emblematic of the higher-level themes we're trying to capture based on the hypothesis. As you become more familiar with specific Financials firms and their industries, you can eventually develop your own strategies. Always be vigilant for firm-specific issues that could cause a stock to act differently than you would expect in the context of your broader strategy.

Recap

We couldn't possibly list every investment strategy out there for the Financials sector. Different strategies will work best at different times. Some will become obsolete. New ones will be discovered. Whatever strategies you choose, always know you could be wrong! Decisions to significantly overweight or underweight an industry relative to the benchmark should be based on a multitude of factors, including an assessment of risk. The point of benchmarking is to properly diversify, so make sure you always have counterstrategies built into your portfolio.

- There are numerous ways to invest in the Financials sector. These include investing in ETFs, indexes or mutual funds or buying the stocks themselves.

- Investors can enhance returns by overweighting and underweighting industries or countries based on a variety of high-level drivers.

- An advanced strategy involves making bets on individual stocks based on specific themes.

Appendix A
Reference Material

Government

The Federal Reserve—America's central bank.
www.federalreserve.gov

The Federal Deposit Insurance Corporation (FDIC) is an independent agency created by the Congress to maintain stability and public confidence in the nation's financial system.
www.fdic.gov

The Treasury Department is the executive agency responsible for promoting economic prosperity and ensuring the financial security of the US.
www.treasury.gov

The Consumer Financial Protection Bureau (CFPB) has the central mission of making markets for consumer financial products and services work for Americans.
www.consumerfinance.gov

The National Association of Insurance Commissioners (NAIC) is the US standard-setting and regulatory support organization created and governed by the chief insurance regulators from the 50 states, the District of Columbia and 5 US territories.
www.naic.org

The European Central Bank (ECB) is the central bank for Europe's single currency, the euro. The ECB's main task is maintaining the euro's purchasing power and thus price stability in the euro area.
www.ecb.int

The European Banking Authority (EBA) officially came into being as of January 1, 2011, and has taken over all existing and ongoing tasks and responsibilities from the Committee of European Banking Supervisors (CEBS). The EBA acts as a hub-and-spoke network of EU and national bodies safeguarding public values such as the stability of the financial system, the transparency of markets and financial products and the protection of depositors and investors.
www.eba.europa.eu/

The Financial Services Authority (FSA) is the regulator of the financial services industry in the UK.
www.fsa.gov.uk

The Bank of England is the central bank of the UK.
www.bankofengland.co.uk

The European Commission is the EU's executive body and represents the interests of Europe as a whole (as opposed to the interests of individual countries).
ec.europa.eu/index_en.htm

The Website for the **European Union**.
europa.eu/index_en.htm

The Bank of Japan (BOJ) is Japan's central bank.
www.boj.or.jp/en/

Global Organizations

The Bank for International Settlements (BIS) has a mission of serving central banks in their pursuit of monetary and financial stability, fostering international cooperation in those areas and acting as a bank for central banks.
www.bis.org

The International Monetary Fund (IMF) is an organization of 187 countries working to foster global monetary cooperation, secure financial stability, facilitate international trade, promote high employment and sustainable economic growth and reduce poverty around the world.
www.imf.org

The World Bank is a source of financial and technical assistance to developing countries around the world.
www.worldbank.org ·

The Organisation for Economic Co-operation and Development (OECD) promotes policies that will improve the economic and social well-being of people around the world.
www.oecd.org

Industry Organizations

International Swaps and Derivatives Association, Inc. (ISDA) is a global trade association for OTC derivatives and maintains industry-standard ISDA documentation.
www.isda.org

The Depository Trust & Clearing Corporation (DTCC), through its subsidiaries, provides clearing, settlement and information services for equities, corporate and municipal bonds, government and mortgage-backed securities, money market instruments and over-the-counter derivatives.
www.dtcc.com

The BBA is the leading trade association for the UK banking and financial services sector.
www.bba.org.uk

Euribor-EBF is an international non-profit-making association under Belgian law founded in 1999 with the launch of the euro and based in Brussels (10, rue Montoyer, 1000 Brussels). Its members are national banking associations in the member states of the European Union that are involved in the euro-zone and the euro-system.
euribor-ebf.eu

Founded in 1875, the **American Bankers Association** (ABA) represents banks of all sizes and charters and is the voice for the nation's $13 trillion banking industry and its 2 million employees.
www.aba.com

The Mortgage Bankers Association (MBA) is the national association representing the real estate finance industry, an industry that employs more than 280,000 people in virtually every community in the country.

www.mbaa.org

The Securities Industry and Financial Markets Association (SIFMA) brings together the shared interests of hundreds of securities firms, banks and asset managers. These companies are engaged in communities across the country to raise capital for businesses, promote job creation and lead economic growth.

www.sifma.org

The Asia Securities Industry & Financial Markets Association (ASIFMA) is a broadly based professional advocacy organization that seeks to promote the growth and development of Asia's capital markets and facilitate their orderly integration into the global financial system.

www.asifma.org/

The Association for Financial Markets in Europe (AFME) is the voice of Europe's wholesale financial markets. It represents the leading global and European banks and other significant capital markets players.

www.afme.eu/

The Independent Directors Council (IDC) serves the mutual fund independent director community and provides a venue for advancing the education, communication and policy positions of mutual fund independent directors. The IDC's Governing Council consists of 21 independent directors. The Council extends to all directors an invitation to participate in the programs and activities offered by the Independent Directors Council.

www.ici.org

The World Federation of Exchanges (WFE) is the trade association of 54 publicly regulated stock, futures and options

exchanges. Its market operators are responsible for the functioning of key components in the financial world.
www.world-exchanges.org

The American Insurance Association (AIA) is the leading property-casualty insurance trade organization, representing approximately 300 insurers that write more than $117 billion in premiums each year.
www.aiadc.org

The American Council of Life Insurers (ACLI) represents more than 300 legal reserve life insurer and fraternal benefit society member companies operating in the United States.
www.acli.com

The International Association of Insurance Supervisors (IAIS) represents insurance regulators and supervisors of some 190 jurisdictions in nearly 140 countries, constituting 97% of the world's insurance premiums. It also has more than 120 observers.
www.iaisweb.org

The Institute of International Finance, Inc. (IIF) is the world's only global association of financial institutions.
www.iif.com

The Japanese Bankers Association (JBA) is a premier financial organization whose members consist of banks, bank holding companies and bankers' associations in Japan.
www.zenginkyo.or.jp/en/

Appendix B
Derivatives

Many Diversified Financials, Insurance and Banking companies use *derivatives* to alter the characteristics of assets, to hedge risks and to take bets. This often makes their balance sheets difficult to digest because you can't take the numbers at face value. For example, an investment bank could disclose zero net exposure to Greek sovereign debt, but in reality, it could have $15 billion in gross exposure and $15 billion in insurance on the exposure, which collectively nets to zero. Other common tactics include altering cash flows via interest rate contracts or hedging currency risk with foreign currency swaps.

At face value, the derivatives market is the largest market in the world. As of November 2011, the estimated notional value of over $707 trillion dwarfs the combined value of the $56.5 trillion global stock market and $98.7 trillion global bond market.[1] Considering the complex nature of derivatives, this may seem daunting, but the reality is $707 trillion is a useless number. Here's why.

INTEREST RATE CONTRACTS

The vast majority of the derivatives market consists of interest rate contracts. For the most part, these contracts simply swap cash flows— fixed for variable. There is no risk to principal, and no money changes hands other than the difference between cash flows at the end of the contractual period. The large notional value simply represents the principal amount used to determine the contracted cash flows.

For example, you may want to swap the 2.50% fixed rate on a $10 million US Treasury note for a variable rate—let's assume 2.49%.

If rates didn't move over the 10-year period, the total money changing hands would be the difference between 2.50% and 2.49% over the 10-year period (around $1,000 per year). But the notional amount of the contract would be $10 million, vastly overstating the potential impact of the contract.

In 2011, interest rate contracts had a notional value of $553 trillion, but the market value of these contracts amassed to just $14.6 trillion—only 3% of the notional value.[2] Although $14 trillion is still a large number, even this is overstated since the *gross credit exposures* of total over-the-counter derivatives is just $3.5 trillion—gross notional takes into account bilateral netting agreements.[3] This implies the interest rate swap market is valued closer to just $2 trillion.[4]

Definition: Over the Counter (OTC)

Over the counter refers to securities transactions not on an exchange.

To varying degrees, other types of derivatives follow a similar pattern. There is the notional value, which is the value from which derivatives derive their values—hence the name. There is the market value, which is the replacement cost of the contracts. And then there is the credit exposure, which is net of legally enforceable bilateral netting agreements. Table B.1 shows the various types and values of the global derivatives market in June 2011.

CREDIT DEFAULT SWAPS

Imagine you were a bank and had a $100 million loan portfolio, which we will simply refer to as an asset. This asset contains an element of credit risk, and for some reason, you don't want to be exposed to the credit risk (risk of default) anymore. But you can't sell the asset—perhaps due to an illiquid market or because you're bound

Table B.1   Global Derivatives Market

Futures & Options	Notional Amount Outstanding	Gross Market Value	Gross Credit Exposure*
Interest rate contracts	$ 553,880	$13,244	$2,016*
Foreign exchange contracts	$ 64,698	$2,336	$356*
Unallocated	$46,543	$1,414	$215*
Credit default swaps	$32,409	$1,345	$205*
Equity-linked contracts	$6,841	$708	$108*
Commodity contracts	$3,197	$471	$72*
Total	$707,569	$19,518	$2,971

*Estimated using BIS data

Source: Bank for International Settlements, "OTC Derivatives Market Activity in the First Half of 2011" (November 16, 2011): www.bis.org/publ/otc_hy1111.htm.

by contract. Since you can't sell, instead, you can purchase an insurance contract on the asset, protecting you from the credit risk.

With the insurance, if your asset defaults, the insurance company would indemnify you (make you whole). The cost of this insurance is an annual fee, but you're more than happy paying the fee if you're protected against default. This process, as a whole, is a credit default swap (CDS)—an insurance contract against a credit event.

Let's say a year later, you decide you no longer want the credit protection, but you're bound by the CDS agreement. Instead of attempting to sell the contract (which isn't possible in many cases due to the unique nature of many contracts) or potentially paying a fee to back out of the deal, you enter into an offsetting agreement. Instead of buying insurance, you sell insurance *on the same asset*. This way, your long position offsets your short position, and your net exposure is that of your original position.

Unlike interest rate swaps, CDS do have a larger degree of credit risk associated with them since principal values are at risk, not just cash flows. In the same example, let's say there was a credit event, your asset defaulted and the recovery value was 50%. Your counterparty to the CDS contract would be responsible for making you whole—either by taking possession of the asset and indemnifying you or by giving you the difference between the asset's original value and the recovery value.

But what if your counterparty can't make good on that obligation? You lose! Sure, you can take legal action against the counterparty, but if the counterparty defaulted on his obligation, it's likely because he's already in a bad situation. This is why it's more important to pay attention to counterparty risk in the CDS market than in the interest rate swap market. If your counterparty in the interest rate market defaults, you are simply out a certain degree of cash flow, which can hurt. But if your CDS counterparty defaults, you could be out a large sum of principal, which can be devastating. Moreover, if you're using the CDS to alter the risk characteristics of your asset for regulatory capital purposes, things get even trickier. (Read more on the risk weighting of assets in Chapter 2.)

OTHER

Foreign exchange-, commodity- and equity-linked contracts are much less mysterious than CDS or interest rate swaps. They are contracts allowing for hedging or betting on the direction of currencies, commodities or equities.

Appendix C
Risk-Adjusted Balance Sheet

Basel offers three approaches to calculating risk-adjusted assets: an internal ratings approach (in which each bank will use its own calculations and assumptions), the Standardized approach and the Simplified Standardized Approach, which offers the simplest options for calculating risk-weighted assets. The Standardized approach, the most commonly used, uses external credit assessments from agencies such as Standard and Poor's. Table C.1 provides a general overview of various weighting schemes under the standardized risk weighting approach as of June 2011. Tables C.2 and C.3 provide the associated weighting schemes for sovereigns, banks and corporates.

These risk weightings can influence the amount of capital a bank is required to hold. Consider the numerous sovereign downgrades in Europe during 2011 and 2012. With sovereign bonds generally comprising a large portion of bank balance sheets, each downgrade can be meaningful if it triggers a higher risk weighting. There is a lot of fine print to the calculations, but in general, if there are more than two credit ratings, the two highest ratings will be used to determine the risk weight.

Table C.1   Standardized Risk Weighting Approach

Risk Adjustments for Claims on...	Standardized
Sovereigns and central banks	0–150% based on external credit assessment (See Table C.2.)
Other official entities	Select entities receive 0%, others treated as banks
Banks and securities firms	Either 1 notch lower than sovereign risk or based on external assessment of the bank (See Table C.2.)
Corporates	20–100% based on external credit assessment (See Table C.3.)
Retail portfolios	75%
Residential property	35%
Commercial property	100%
Past-due loans	100–150% based on level of provisions and type
Higher risk categories	150%
Off-balance sheet items	Equivalent to credit exposure or range 0–100%
Other assets	100%

Source: BIS http://www.bis.org/publ/bcbsca04.pdf (July 2011)

Table C.2   Standardized Risk Weightings—Sovereigns and Banks

Sovereign External Credit Assessment	Sovereign External Credit Assessment	Bank External Credit Assessment—Option 2
AAA to AA−	0%	20%
A+ to A−	20%	50%
BBB+ to BBB−	50%	50%
BB+ to B−	100%	100%
<B−	150%	150%
Unrated	100%	50%

Source: BIS http://www.bis.org/publ/bcbsca04.pdf (July 2011)

Table C.3   Standardized Risk Weightings— Corporates

AAA to AA−	20%
A+ to A−	50%
BBB+ to BB−	100%
<BB−	150%
Unrated	100%

Source: BIS http://www.bis.org/publ/bcbsca04.pdf (July 2011)

Notes

Chapter 1: Financials Basics

1. Thomson Reuters; MSCI World Index, as of 12/31/2011.
2. Ibid.
3. MSCI. The MSCI information may only be used for your internal use, may not be reproduced or redisseminated in any form and may not be used to create any financial instruments or products or any indices. The MSCI information is provided on an "as is" basis and the user of this information assumes the entire risk of any use made of this information. MSCI, each of its affiliates and each other person involved in or related to compiling, computing or creating any MSCI information (collectively, the "MSCI Parties") expressly disclaims all warranties (including, without limitation, any warranties of originality, accuracy, completeness, timeliness, non-infringement, merchantability and fitness for a particular purpose) with respect to this information. Without limiting any of the foregoing, in no event shall any MSCI Party have any liability for any direct, indirect, special, incidental, punitive, consequential (including, without limitation, lost profits) or any other damages.
4. Ibid.
5. Thomson Reuters; MSCI World Index, as of 12/31/2010.
6. Thomson Reuters; Global Financial Data, Inc., from 12/31/1974 to 12/31/2011.
7. Thomson Reuters, from 12/31/1974 to 12/31/2011.
8. Thomson Reuters, as of 12/31/2011.
9. See note 3.
10. Global Financial Data, Inc.; US Federal Reserve, from 12/31/1989 to 12/31/2010.
11. Thomson Reuters, from 12/31/1969 to 12/31/2011.
12. Ibid.
13. See note 3.
14. See note 8.
15. See note 3.
16. See note 8.
17. Bank for International Settlements, "Securities Statistics and Syndicated Loans" (12/31/2011), www.bis.org/statistics/secstats.htm (accessed 03/27/2012).
18. Bank of America Merrill Lynch, as of 12/31/2011.
19. See note 3.

Chapter 2: Banks

1. Thomson Reuters, as of 12/31/2011.
2. MSCI. The MSCI information may only be used for your internal use, may not be reproduced or redisseminated in any form and may not be used to create any financial instruments or products or any indices. The MSCI information is provided on an "as is" basis and the user of this information assumes the entire risk of any use made of this information. MSCI, each of its affiliates and each other person involved in or related to compiling, computing or creating any MSCI information (collectively, the "MSCI Parties") expressly disclaims all warranties (including, without limitation, any warranties of originality, accuracy, completeness, timeliness, non-infringement, merchantability and fitness for a particular purpose) with respect to this information. Without limiting any of the foregoing, in no event shall any MSCI Party have any liability for any direct, indirect, special, incidental, punitive, consequential (including, without limitation, lost profits) or any other damages.
3. International Monetary Fund, "Central Bank Balances and Reserve Requirements" (February 2011) www.imf.org/external/pubs/ft/wp/2011/wp1136.pdf (accessed 03/27/2012).
4. Federal Deposit Insurance Corporation, "Quarterly Banking Profile," as of 12/31/2010. Big assets = >$10b and small = $100m–$1B.
5. Bloomberg Finance L.P., as of 12/31/2011.
6. Ibid.
7. See note 1.
8. Ibid.
9. Ibid.
10. See note 2.
11. Thomson Reuters, from 12/31/2004 to 12/31/2011.
12. Ibid.
13. See note 2.
14. Federal Deposit Insurance Corporation, as of 12/31/2011.
15. Bank for International Settlements, "Basel III: A Global Regulatory Framework for More Resilient Banks and Banking Systems" (December 2010, rev. June 2011), www.bis.org/publ/bcbs189.htm (accessed March 28, 2012).
16. Federal Deposit Insurance Corporation, "Quarterly Banking Profile," as of 12/31/2010.

Chapter 3: Diversified Financials

1. MSCI. The MSCI information may only be used for your internal use, may not be reproduced or redisseminated in any form and may not be used to create any financial instruments or products or any indices. The MSCI information is provided on an "as is" basis and the user of this information assumes the entire risk of any use made of this information. MSCI, each of its affiliates and each other person involved in or related to compiling, computing or creating any MSCI information (collectively, the "MSCI Parties") expressly disclaims all warranties (including, without limitation, any warranties of originality, accuracy, completeness, timeliness, non-infringement, merchantability and fitness for a particular purpose) with respect to this information. Without limiting any of the foregoing, in no event shall any MSCI Party have any liability for any direct,

indirect, special, incidental, punitive, consequential (including, without limitation, lost profits) or any other damages.

2. State Street, Bank of New York Mellon, and Northern Trust Company 2011 10-Ks.
3. Goldman Sachs and Morgan Stanley Company 2011 10-Ks.
4. Bloomberg Finance L.P., as of 12/31/2011.
5. Ibid.
6. US Federal Reserve, "Consumer Credit" (January 2012), www.federalreserve.gov /releases/g19/current/default.htm (accessed March 28, 2012).
7. Ibid.
8. SLM Corporation 2010 Annual Report.
9. See note 4.
10. Bloomberg Finance L.P.; US Bureau of Labor Statistics, as of 12/31/2011.
11. Thomson Reuters; MSCI. The MSCI information may only be used for your internal use, may not be reproduced or redisseminated in any form and may not be used to create any financial instruments or products or any indices. The MSCI information is provided on an "as is" basis and the user of this information assumes the entire risk of any use made of this information. MSCI, each of its affiliates and each other person involved in or related to compiling, computing or creating any MSCI information (collectively, the "MSCI Parties") expressly disclaims all warranties (including, without limitation, any warranties of originality, accuracy, completeness, timeliness, non-infringement, merchantability and fitness for a particular purpose) with respect to this information. Without limiting any of the foregoing, in no event shall any MSCI Party have any liability for any direct, indirect, special, incidental, punitive, consequential (including, without limitation, lost profits) or any other damages. As of 12/31/2011.
12. Ibid.
13. Company 10-Ks, as of 12/31/2011.
14. US Federal Reserve, "Flow of Funds Accounts of the United States" (March 8, 2012), www.federalreserve.gov/releases/z1/Current/ (accessed March 28, 2012).
15. Thomson Reuters, as of 12/31/2011.

Chapter 4: Insurance Industry Group

1. Thomson Reuters, as of 12/31/2011.
2. National Association of Insurance Commissioners, "NAIC Industry Overview State of the Insurance Industry" (2011). Defined by premiums. www.naic.org/documents/fin _summit_pres_10_industry_overview.pdf (accessed March 27, 2012).
3. MSCI. The MSCI information may only be used for your internal use, may not be reproduced or redisseminated in any form and may not be used to create any financial instruments or products or any indices. The MSCI information is provided on an "as is" basis and the user of this information assumes the entire risk of any use made of this information. MSCI, each of its affiliates and each other person involved in or related to compiling, computing or creating any MSCI information (collectively, the "MSCI Parties") expressly disclaims all warranties (including, without limitation, any warranties of originality, accuracy, completeness, timeliness, non-infringement, merchantability and fitness for a particular purpose) with respect to this information. Without limiting any of the foregoing, in no event shall any MSCI Party have any liability for any direct,

indirect, special, incidental, punitive, consequential (including, without limitation, lost profits) or any other damages.

4. A.M. Best, *The Guide to Understanding the Insurance Industry*, 2009–2010.

5. Ibid.

6. ACLI, "ACLI Life Insurers Fact Book 2010" (October 10, 2010), www.acli.com/Tools /Industry%20Facts/Life%20Insurers%20Fact%20Book/Pages/GR10-242.aspx (accessed March 28, 2012).

7. US Federal Reserve, "Flow of Funds Accounts of the United States: Flows and Out-standings Second Quarter 2011" (September 16, 2011), www.federalreserve.gov /releases/z1/20110916/z1.pdf (accessed March 28, 2012).

8. US Census Bureau, "Table 120. Deaths and Death Rates by Selected Causes: 2006 and 2007" (May 2007), www.census.gov/compendia/statab/2012/tables/12s0120.pdf (accessed March 27, 2012).

9. Bloomberg Finance L.P., as of 12/31/2011.

10. Capgemini, "2007 World Insurance Report" (2007), www.efma.com/wir07/pdf/WIR _Roadshow_London.pdf (accessed March 28, 2012).

11. American Insurance Association, "Insurance 201: Property-Casualty Finance," *AIA Advocate* (September 2006), www.aiadc.org/AIAdotNET/docHandler.aspx?DocID= 298116 (accessed March 28, 2012).

12. TheCityUK, "Financial Market Series: Fund Management" (October 2011), www.thec-ityuk.com/assets/Uploads/Fund-Management-2011.pdf (accessed March 28, 2012).

13. Thomson Reuters; S&P 500 Insurance Index, as of December 2006.

14. Rodney Lester, "Introduction to the Insurance Industry," The World Bank (March 2009), http://siteresources.worldbank.org/EXTFINANCIALSECTOR /Resources/282884-1242281415644/Introduction_to_Insurance_Industry.pdf (accessed March 29, 2012).

15. Ibid.

16. International Association of Insurance Supervisors, "Insurance Core Principles, Standards, Guidance and Assessment Methodology" (October 2011).

Chapter 5: Real Estate Industry Group

1. "The Future Size of the Global Real Estate Market," RREEF Research (July 2007), www.rreef.com/content/_media/Research_The_Future_Size_of_The_Global_Real _Estate_Market_July_2007.pdf (accessed 03/27/2012).

2. Thomson Reuters; MSCI World Index, as of 12/31/2011.

3. MSCI. The MSCI information may only be used for your internal use, may not be reproduced or redisseminated in any form and may not be used to create any financial instruments or products or any indices. The MSCI information is provided on an "as is" basis and the user of this information assumes the entire risk of any use made of this information. MSCI, each of its affiliates and each other person involved in or related to compiling, computing or creating any MSCI information (collectively, the "MSCI Parties") expressly disclaims all warranties (including, without limitation, any warranties of originality, accuracy, completeness, timeliness, non-infringement, merchantability and fitness for a particular purpose) with respect to this information. Without limiting any of the foregoing, in no event shall any MSCI Party have any liability for any direct,

indirect, special, incidental, punitive, consequential (including, without limitation, lost profits) or any other damages.

4. Bloomberg Finance L.P., as of 03/20/2012.
5. Thomson Reuters, Russell 2000 Value Index, as of 12/31/2011.
6. Bloomberg Finance L.P., as of 03/20/2012.
7. See note 3.
8. Thomson Reuters, S&P 500 and FTSE NAREIT All REIT Indexes, total return in USD, as of 12/31/2011.
9. Thomson Reuters, as of 12/31/2010.
10. Annaly Capital Management 2011 10-K; Bloomberg Finance L.P., as of 12/31/2011.
11. Annaly Capital Management 2011 10-K.

Chapter 6: The Top-Down Method

1. Matthew Kalman, "Einstein Letters Reveal a Turmoil Beyond Science," *Boston Globe* (July 11, 2006), www.boston.com/news/world/middleeast/articles/2006/07/11/einstein_letters_reveal_a_turmoil_beyond_science/ (accessed March 30, 2012).
2. Michael Michalko, "Combinatory Play," Creative Thinking, www.creativethinking.net /DT10_CombinatoryPlay.htm?Entry=Good (accessed March 30, 2012).
3. Gary P. Brinson, Brian D. Singer, and Gilbert L. Beebower, "Determinants of Portfolio Performance II: An Update," *The Financial Analysts Journal* 47 (1991), 3.
4. Source: MSCI. The MSCI information may only be used for your internal use, may not be reproduced or redisseminated in any form and may not be used to create any financial instruments or products or any indices. The MSCI information is provided on an "as is" basis and the user of this information assumes the entire risk of any use made of this information. MSCI, each of its affiliates and each other person involved in or related to compiling, computing or creating any MSCI information (collectively, the "MSCI Parties") expressly disclaims all warranties (including, without limitation, any warranties of originality, accuracy, timeliness, non-infringement, merchantability and fitness for a particular purpose) with respect to this information. Without limiting any of the foregoing, in no event shall any MSCI Party have any liability for any direct, indirect, special, incidental, punitive, consequential (including, without limitation, lost profits) or any other damages.
5. Ibid.
6. See note 4.
7. Thomson Reuters, Financials weight in the MSCI World Index as of 04/30/2012.
8. See note 4.
9. Ibid.
10. Ibid.

Appendix B: Derivatives

1. Bank for International Settlements, "Securities Statistics and Syndicated Loans" (March 2012), www.bis.org/statistics/secstats.htm (accessed March 30, 2012); World Federation of Exchanges Monthly Statistics, as of 12/31/2011, http://world-exchanges.org/statistics/monthly-reports (accessed March 30, 2012); Bank for International Settlements,

"OTC Derivatives Market Activity in the First Half of 2011" (November 16, 2011), www.bis.org/publ/otc_hy1111.htm (accessed March 30, 2012).

2. Bank for International Settlements, "OTC Derivatives Market Activity in the First Half of 2011" (November 16, 2011), www.bis.org/publ/otc_hy1111.htm (accessed March 30, 2012).

3. Ibid.

4. See note 2.

About the Author

Jarred J. Kriz (Camas, Washington) has been in the financial services industry since 1997, with experience in the banking, investment banking, brokerage and asset management fields. He regularly presents to audiences at investing workshops across the country and currently works as a Senior Capital Markets Research Analyst at Fisher Investments with a focus on the Financials Sector and macroeconomic strategy. Originally from Simi Valley, California, he now resides in Camas, Washington, with his wife, Dawn; his son, Shawn; and two daughters, Evelyn and Madelyn.

Index

Accounting issues
  fair value accounting
    (mark-to-market), 50, 51
  insurance expenses, amortization
    of, 88
  insurance unearned premiums, 90
  REITs, 118–120
Allowance ratio (loan loss reserve to
  total loans), 43
American International Group
  (AIG), 94
Annaly Capital Management (NLY),
  112–114
Annuities, 85, 87, 88, 96, 97
Asian Contagion, 9, 16, 17, 48, 52
Asset allocation, 128
Asset Managers, 64–68, 148
Assets and liabilities
  assets defined, 5
  banks, 35
  insurance industry, 86–90
  sensitivities, 44, 154
Assets-to-equity ratio (assets/equity),
  15, 16
Assets under custody (AUC), 69
Assets under management (AUM), 65,
  66, 68
Auto insurance, 86, 98. *See also*
  Insurance industry
Auto loans, 76, 79, 80. *See also*
  Consumer Finance

Bancassurance, 89
Bank of America, 33, 46, 63, 80
Bank of America Merrill Lynch Global
  Broad Market Index, 27, 28
Bank of NY Mellon, 69
Banks
  asset sensitivity, 44
  assets and liabilities, 35
  capital conservation buffer, 55
  capital ratios, 54, 55
  CD rates, 60, 61
  characteristics of industry group,
    48–53
  commoditization of financial
    services, 44
  core funding, 59, 61
  countercyclical buffer, 55
  credit metrics, 43, 44
  credit quality, 41–44
  cross-selling, 41
  deposit funding, 59
  described, 35
  diversified, 33, 34, 45, 47, 162
  dividends, 49, 50
  economic conditions, sensitivity to,
    52, 53
  efficiency ratio, 41
  and employment trends, 52, 53
  fractional reserve banking
    system, 35
  global liquidity standards, 56

Banks (*continued*)
  going concern and gone concern
    capital, 54
  industry breakdown, 24, 33, 45
  interbank lending, 60
  and interest rates, 16, 17, 40, 52
  investment banks. *See* Investment
    Banks (IBs)
  leverage, 50, 51
  leverage ratios, 16, 55, 56
  liability sensitivity, 44
  liquidity, 56, 59–61
  liquidity ratios, 56
  mega banks, 33
  money center banks, 45
  money multiplication, 36–38
  mortgage finance companies, 33, 45
  net interest income (NII), 38–40
  net interest margin (NIM), 38, 40, 49
  non-interest-bearing deposits, 61
  non-interest income, 38, 40, 41
  performance, 48–53
  publicly traded, size rankings, 46
  regional, 33, 34, 45–47, 162
  regulation of, 53–61
  regulatory capital, 54
  required reserve ratio (RRR), 35–37
  residential loans, 52
  risk-adjusted balance sheets, 54, 55
  role of, 33, 34
  sensitivity to economic conditions,
    52, 53
  size, 48, 49
  super-regional, 45, 47
  thrifts, 33, 45
  types of, 45–48
  up-selling, 41
  value versus growth, 49, 50
  volatility, 50–52
  weight in various benchmarks, 33, 34
  wholesale funding, 59

Basel Accords
  Basel Committee, 53, 54
  Basel II, 54
  Basel III, 54–59, 101
Bear markets
  and asset managers, 65
  and banks, 48
  Financials sector, 8, 13, 19, 20, 160
  and insurance products, 97
  and REITs, 111
  and top-down processes, 128
Benchmarks
  bank weighting in various
    benchmarks, 33, 34
  described, 24, 25, 128, 129
  Financials sector benchmarks, 5,
    24–27, 131
  Financials sector compared to other
    sectors, 25
  fixed income, 27–29
  global financials, 24–27
  insurance weighting in various
    benchmarks, 84–86
  MSCI Indexes. *See* MSCI
  NAREIT REIT Indexes, 109–111,
    113
  overweighting and underweighting,
    25, 29, 114, 129, 132, 139–142,
    144, 160–162, 164
  real estate, weighting in various
    benchmarks, 103, 104, 107,
    108, 113
  Russell 2000. *See* Russell 2000
  sector benchmarks, 29
  small-cap, 25, 103, 104. *See also*
    Russell 2000
  S&P 500. *See* S&P 500
  and top-down method of investing,
    128–131, 139–141, 160
Beta
  described, 10–13

insurance industry, 94, 95
yield/beta ratio, 157
Bond indexes, 28
Bonds, 27–29
Book value, 14, 49, 118, 119
Bottom-up investing, 126–128
Brand equity, 155, 156
Brokers
    Capital Markets industry, 64, 70,
        74, 75
    insurance industry, 83, 94, 95
    and interest rates, 16
Bull markets
    and banks, 48
    financial sector, 19, 20, 160
    and insurance products, 97
    and REITs, 111
    and top-down processes, 128
Business and earnings drivers,
    145–147
Business strategy, 147, 148, 155

Capex efficiency ratio, 157
Capital conservation buffer, 55
Capital expenditures (capex), 156, 157
Capital markets, 10, 23, 63, 64, 69, 70,
    75, 87, 94, 129
Capital Markets industry
    Asset Managers, 64–68
    Brokers, 64, 70, 74, 75
    Custody Banks, 64, 65, 69
    Diversified Investment Banking, 64
    industry breakdown, 24, 63, 64
    Investment Banking, 16, 64, 70–74
Capital ratios, 54, 55, 99
Capitalization rate (cap rate), 118, 120
CD rates, 60, 61
Citigroup, 33, 46, 63, 80
Client execution, 71, 72
Combinatory play, 126
Combined ratio, 91, 92

Commoditization of financial services,
    44, 75, 89, 90
Competition and competitive
    advantage, 44, 92, 138, 145, 147,
    148, 155
Consumer credit. *See* Consumer
    Finance
Consumer Finance, 24, 63, 64, 76–80
Consumer spending, 52, 78, 115, 163
Core funding, 59, 61
Core funding ratio, 61
Correlation, 11–13
Countercyclical buffer, 55
Country, sector, size and style decisions,
    128–130, 132–136
Credit metrics, 43, 44
Credit quality
    and Asset Managers, 66
    banks, 41–44
Credit ratings
    agencies, 156
    insurance companies, 99, 100
Credit risk, 53, 55, 87, 114
Credit Suisse, 75
Cross-selling, 41
Custody Banks, 64, 65, 69

Debt service ratio (DSR), 79
Deferred Acquisition Expenses
    (DAE), 88
Deferred Policy Acquisition Cost
    (DAC), 88, 97
Deposit funding, banks, 59
Deutsche Bank, 33, 75
Distribution platforms, insurance, 89
Diversified banks, 33, 34, 45, 47, 162
Diversified Capital Markets, 64, 75
Diversified Financial Services, 64, 80, 81
Diversified Financials industry
    Asset Managers, 64–68
    Brokers, 64, 74, 75

Diversified Financials industry
(*continued*)
Capital Markets, 63–75
Consumer Finance, 24, 63, 64,
76–80
Custody Banks, 64, 65, 69
described, 63
Diversified Capital Markets, 64, 75
Diversified Financial Services, 64,
80, 81
Diversified Investment Banking, 64
industry breakdown, 24, 63, 64
Investment Banks (IBs), 16, 64,
70–74
weight in MSCI ACWI, 63
Diversified Investment Banking, 64
Diversified REITs, 108, 116, 118
Dividend yield (DY), 14, 50, 108, 109,
152, 156, 157
Dividends
banks, 49, 50
investment income, 93
REITs, 107–109, 111
value versus growth companies, 14, 49
Dodd-Frank Act, 72, 100
Domestic investing, 4
DownREIT, 106
Duration, defined, 19

Earned premiums, 89. *See also*
Insurance industry
Earnings growth, 14, 108, 156, 157
Earnings variability, 154
Economic conditions, sensitivity to,
52, 53
Efficiency ratio, 41
Einstein, Albert, 124–126
Emerging markets
banks, 49
and commodity demand, 134

indexes, 4, 25, 29, 34, 64, 85, 108
insurance industry in, 95, 98
Employment trends, 52, 53
Enterprise value to earnings before
interest, taxes, depreciation and
amortization ratio (EV/EBITDA),
152
Equity REITs, 107, 111, 112, 115–118
EURIBOR, 60
Exchange-traded funds (ETFs),
139, 161
Expense ratio, 91, 92

Fair value accounting, 50, 51
Fee income, insurance industry, 89, 93
FICC (fixed income, currencies and
commodities), 71, 72
Financial Accounting Standards, FAS
157 (fair value accounting), 50, 51
Financial crisis of 2008-2009
and banks, 10, 13, 17, 37, 39, 40,
50, 52, 54, 56, 59, 72
and insurance companies, 94, 98
and mortgage-backed securities,
112–114
Financial obligations ratio (FOR), 79
Financial strength, 156
Financials sector overview
balance sheets, 5
bear markets, 8, 13, 19, 20, 160. *See
also* Bear markets
benchmarks, 5, 24–27, 131. *See also*
Benchmarks
beta, 10–13
bull markets, 19, 20, 160
characteristics of, 4–23
complexity, 3
cyclical versus defensive, 5, 19–22
ETFs, 139, 161
fixed income benchmarks, 27–29

global benchmarks, 24–27
Global Industry Classification
    Standard (GICS), 23, 24
importance of, 3, 4
income statements, 5, 6
industry groups, industry, and sub-
    industry breakdowns, 23, 24. *See
    also* Industry breakdown
interest rate sensitivity, 5, 16–19
investing strategies, 159–164
leverage, 5, 15, 16
other people's money (OPM),
    reliance on, 5, 23
performance, 7–9, 16
regulatory environment, 3–5, 22, 23.
    See also Regulatory compliance
sector benchmarks, 29
security analysis, 153–157
size of, 3, 5, 6, 26
top-down investing in Financials. *See*
    Top-down method of investing
value versus growth orientation, 4,
    13–15
volatility. *See* Volatility
weight, 7
Fixed income, currencies and
    commodities (FICC), 71, 72
Fixed income benchmarks, 27–29
Float cycle, 87, 90
Fractional reserve banking system, 35
Fundamental and stock price
    performance analysis, 145,
    149, 150
Funds from operations (FFO), 118–120

General insurance, 86
Geographic diversity, 155
Global financial benchmarks, 24–27
Global Industry Classification Standard
    (GICS), 23, 24

Global investing, 4
Global liquidity standards, banks, 56
Global systemically important banks
    (G-SIBs), 80
Going concern capital, 54
Gone concern capital, 54

Hard and soft markets, insurance
    industry, 90, 91
Hedging, 73
Hybrid REITs, 107

Indemnification, defined, 83
Industrial REITs, 107, 108, 115, 117
Industry breakdown
    Banks, 24, 33, 45
    Diversified Financials, 24, 63, 64
    Global Industry Classification
        Standards (GICS), 23, 24
    Insurance, 24, 83, 84
    Real Estate, 24, 103, 107, 108
Insurance Core Principles (ICPs), 101
Insurance industry
    annuities, 88, 96, 97
    assets and liabilities, 86–90
    auto insurance, 98
    bancassurance, 89
    beta, 94, 95
    brokers, 83, 94, 95
    characteristics of insurers, 84–89
    combined ratio, 91, 92
    credit ratings, 99–100
    credit risk, 87
    Deferred Acquisition Expenses
        (DAE), 88
    Deferred Policy Acquisition Cost
        (DAC), 88, 97
    distribution platforms, 89
    drivers, 95
    earned premiums, 89

Insurance industry (*continued*)
  in emerging markets, 95
  expense ratio, 91, 92
  expenses, 88, 93, 94
  fee income, 89, 93
  financial ratios, 99
  float cycle, 87
  float cycle90
  general insurance, 86
  growth, 95, 96
  hard and soft markets, 90, 91
  industry breakdown, 24, 83, 84
  Insurance Core Principles
    (ICPs), 101
  insurance defined, 84
  interest rate risk, 16, 87, 88, 97
  investment portfolios, 87, 92, 93
  Life & Health Insurance (L&H),
    83–85, 87–89, 93, 95–98
  loss ratio, 91, 92
  Multiline Insurers, 83, 94
  net investment income, 89
  net value, 89
  premiums, 84–87, 89–92, 97, 98
  Property & Casualty Insurance
    (P&C), 83, 84, 86–89, 92, 94,
    95, 98
  regulation of, 98–101
  Reinsurance, 83
  revenue sources, 89–94
  risk, 84
  solvency, 89, 91, 99–101
  Solvency II, 100, 101
  underwriting cycle, 90, 91
  underwriting income, 91
  unearned premiums (UEP), 90
  volatility, 94, 95
  weight in benchmarks, 83, 85
  weight in various benchmarks, 84–86
Interbank lending, 60

Interbank offered rate (IBOR), 60
Interest rate sensitivity
  banks, 16, 17, 40, 52
  consumer finance companies, 79, 80
  Financials sector, 5, 16–19, 154
  insurance industry, 16, 87, 88, 97
  real estate industry, 16
  REITs, 108, 111, 114, 117
International Association of Insurance
    Supervisors, 101
Investing strategies
  country level, 159, 161, 162
  industry level, 159, 161, 162
  overview, 159, 160, 164
  sector level, 159–161
  security level, 159, 162, 163
Investment Banks (IBs), 16, 64, 70–74
Investment portfolios
  insurance industry, 87, 92, 93
  management. *See* Portfolio
    management

JP Morgan Chase & Co., 33, 46, 63,
    73, 80

Law of Large Numbers, 84
Leverage
  banks, 15, 16, 50, 51, 55, 56
  Financials sector, 5, 15, 16
Leverage ratios
  banks, 15, 16, 54–56
  and Financials stock selection, 154
Liabilities. *See* Assets and liabilities
LIBOR, 60
Life & Health Insurance (L&H),
    83–85, 87–89, 93, 95–98. *See also*
    Insurance industry
Liquidity, banks, 56, 59–61
Liquidity coverage ratio (LCR), 56
Liquidity ratios, 56, 154

Loan loss reserve to nonperforming loans
    ratio (NPL coverage ratio), 43
Loan loss reserve to total loans ratio
    (allowance ratio), 43
Loan-to-deposit (LDR) ratio, 60,
    61, 154
Loss ratio, 91, 92

Macroeconomic factors, top-down
    method of investing, 128, 129,
    131–136, 160
Margins, 155
Mark-to-market accounting, 50, 51
Market efficiency, 124
Mega banks, 33
Mergers and acquisitions (M&A), 41,
    64, 71, 134, 163
Money center banks, 45
Money multiplication, 36–38
Mortgage-backed securities (MBS),
    112–114
Mortgage REITs, 105, 107, 108,
    111–114
Mortgages
    bank loans, 52
    mortgage finance companies,
        33, 45, 78
MSCI
    AC World Financials, 11, 27
    AC World Sectors Index, 15
    AC World Value Index, 14
    ACWI, 4–6, 26, 27, 34, 63, 69
    EAFE, 25, 29, 34, 64, 85, 108
    EM, 25, 29, 34, 64, 85, 108
    World Financials Index, 11, 131,
        139–142
    World Index, 4, 10–12, 25, 29, 34,
        48, 49, 64, 80–81, 85, 104, 108,
        129–131
    World Industry Index, 51

Multiline Insurers, 83, 94
Mutual funds, 65–68, 112, 161, 164

NAREIT REIT Indexes, 109–111, 113
National Association of Insurance
    Commissioners (NAIC), 100
Nationally recognized statistical rating
    organizations (NRSROs), 63, 80
Net asset value (NAV), 118–120
Net flows measurement, 66
Net interest income (NII), 38–40
Net interest margin (NIM), 38, 40, 49,
    69, 80
Net investment income, 89
Net leverage, 99
Net operating income (NOI),
    118–120
Net stable funding ratio (NSFR), 56
Net value, 89
Newton, Isaac, 125
Non-interest-bearing deposits, 61
Non-interest income, 38, 40, 41
Non-revolving credit, 76
Nonperforming assets to total assets
    ratio (NPA), 43
Nonperforming loans to total loans
    ratio (NPL), 43
Northern Trust, 69

Office REITs, 108, 115, 116
Other people's money (OPM)
    asset managers, role of, 65
    custody banks, role of, 65, 69
    reliance on, 5, 23
Over-the-counter trades (OTC), 71

Pawn shops, 63
Payout ratio, 156
Portfolio drivers, top-down method of
    investing, 129, 132–136, 142

Portfolio management
  benchmarks, 128, 129. *See also*
    Benchmarks
  and investing as a science, 123–126
  top-down method. *See* Top-down
    method of investing
Premium-to-surplus ratio, 99
Premiums, insurance, 84–87, 89–92,
  97, 98. *See also* Insurance
  industry
Price to book ratio (P/B), 49, 137, 152
Price to cash flow ratio (P/CF),
  137, 152
Price-to-earnings (P/E) ratio, 119,
  137, 152
Price-to-FFO ratio (P/FFO), 119
Price to sales ratio (P/S), 137, 152
Private REITs, 105, 106
Pro forma cap rates, 120
Probability of default (POD), 54
Product mix, 154
Property & Casualty Insurance (P&C),
  83, 84, 86–89, 92, 94, 95, 98. *See
  also* Insurance industry
Property prices, 109–111
Public non-listed REITs, 105, 106
Publicly traded banks, size rankings, 46
Publicly traded REITs, 105, 106

R-squared, 11, 16
Real Estate industry
  industry breakdown, 24, 103,
    107, 108
  and interest rates, 16
  Real Estate Investment Trusts
    (REITs). *See* Real Estate
    Investment Trusts (REITs)
  Real Estate Management &
    Development (REMD), 103, 104
  weight in various benchmarks, 103,
    104, 107, 108, 113

Real Estate Investment Trusts (REITs)
  accounting issues, 118–120
  cap rate, 118, 120
  characteristics of, 106, 108–111
  defensive, 109, 111
  defined, 105
  diversified REITs, 108, 116, 118
  dividends, 107–109, 111
  DownREIT, 106
  equity REITs, 107, 111, 112,
    115–118
  funds from operations (FFO),
    118–120
  historical background, 105
  hybrid, 107
  industrial REITs, 107, 108, 115, 117
  interest rate sensitivity, 108, 111,
    114, 117
  mortgage REITs, 105, 107, 108,
    111–114
  net asset value (NAV), 118–120
  net operating income (NOI),
    118–120
  office REITs, 108, 115, 116
  private, 105, 106
  property prices, 109–111
  public non-listed, 105, 106
  publicly-traded, 105, 106
  residential REITs, 107, 108, 115, 117
  retail REITs, 107, 108, 115
  size of, 108
  small cap, 104
  specialized REITs, 108, 118
  sub-industry breakdown, 107, 108
  supply and demand, 109, 110
  tax treatment, 107, 109
  types of, 105, 106
  Umbrella Partnership REIT
    (UPREIT), 106
  value versus growth, 108
  weight in benchmarks, 103, 104

Real Estate Management &
    Development (REMD), 103, 104
Regional banks, 33, 34, 45–47, 162
Regulatory capital, 54
Regulatory compliance
  banks, 53–61
  Consumer Finance companies, 79
  Financials sector regulatory
    environment, 3–5, 22, 23
  insurance industry, 98–101
Reinsurance, 83
Reinvestment, 156, 157
Required reserve ratio (RRR), 35–37
Residential loans. *See* Mortgages
Residential REITs, 107, 108, 115, 117
Retail REITs, 107, 108, 115
Return on equity (ROE), 50
Revenue sources, insurance industry,
    89–94
Revolving credit, 76
Risk
  banks, 35, 39, 42, 43, 52–56, 61
  company-specific, 143, 152–156
  Consumer Finance, 79, 80
  hedging, 73
  identifying, 145, 150–152
  and insurance, 83, 84, 93, 98, 99
  insurance company investment
    portfolios, 87
  interest rate risk, 88
  investment banks, 72–74
  investment risk management, 128,
    129, 131, 137, 139–146,
    150–156, 164
  mortgage-backed securities, 112–114
  political, 156
  REITs, 112–116
  and return, 25, 29, 42
  value at risk (VaR), 74
Risk-adjusted balance sheets, 54, 55
Risk-based capital (RBC) ratio, 99

Russell 2000, 25, 29, 34, 64, 104,
    108, 129
Russell 2000 Financials, 131
Russell Value and Growth Indexes, 108

Sales growth, 154
Sallie Mae (Student Loan Marketing
    Association), 76
Saving trends, 78, 93, 96
Savings & loans (S&Ls), 8, 45, 47
Securities underwriting, 70, 71. *See also*
    Investment Banks (IBs)
Security analysis
  business and earnings drivers (step 1),
    145–147
  Financials sector considerations,
    153–157
  fundamental and stock price
    performance analysis (step 3), 145,
    149, 150
  goal of, 144
  overview, 143
  process, 145–153
  risks, identifying (step 4), 145,
    150–152
  strategic attributes, identifying (step
    2), 145, 147–149
  valuations and consensus
    expectations, analyzing (step 5),
    145, 152, 153
Senior Loan Officer Opinion Survey
    (SLOOS), 39
Shareholder equity, defined, 5
SIBOR, 60
Small cap companies, benchmark index.
    See Russell 2000
Solvency, insurance industry, 89, 91,
    99–101
Solvency II, 100, 101
Solvency ratio, 99
South Sea Bubble, 125

S&P 500, 4, 7, 8, 10–13, 18, 20, 21,
     25, 29, 33, 34, 50, 64, 85, 104,
     109, 111, 128, 129
S&P 500 Financials, 8, 11, 18, 20, 21,
     131, 142
S&P 500 Insurance Index, 94
Specialized REITs, 108, 118
Standard deviation, 9, 10
State Street Bank, 69
Stock selection
     bottom-up investing, 126, 127
     security analysis. *See* Security analysis
     top-down method of investing,
          127–129, 132, 133, 138, 139,
          142–144, 162, 163
Strategic attributes, identifying, 145,
     147–149
Student Loan Marketing Association
     (Sallie Mae), 76
Student loans, 76
Super-regional banks, 45, 47
Supply and demand, 39, 109, 110
Systemically important financial
     institutions (SIFI), 80

Taxation
     annuities, 97
     portfolio drivers, 134, 135
     REITs, 105, 107, 109
Texas ratio, 44
Thrifts, 24, 33, 34, 45, 47
TIBOR, 60
Top-down method of investing
     advantages of, 127, 128
     asset allocation, 128
     benchmarks, use of, 128–131,
          139–141
     bottom-up investing compared, 126,
          127
     country, sector, size and style
          decisions, 128–130, 132–136
     described, 131–139

ETFs, investing in, 139
     macroeconomic factors, 128, 129,
          131–136
     overview, 126, 127, 142, 144
     portfolio drivers, 129, 132–136, 142
     quantitative factor screening, 132,
          136–138
     risk control, 128
     scalability, 127
     70-20-10 allocation, 128
     stock selection, 127–129, 132, 133,
          138, 139, 142–144, 162, 163. *See
          also* Security analysis

UBS, 75
Umbrella Partnership REIT (UPREIT),
     106
Underwriting cycle, 90, 91
Underwriting income, 91
Unearned premiums (UEP), 90
Unemployment rate, 52, 53, 78, 85
Up-selling, 41

Valuation metrics, 49, 152, 153, 157
Valuations and consensus expectations,
     analyzing, 145, 152, 153
Value at Risk (VaR), 74
Value investing, 9, 108, 124
Value versus growth, 4, 13–15, 49, 50,
     108
Volatility
     banks, 50–52
     Financials sector, 4, 7–13
     insurance industry, 94, 95
Volcker Rule, 72, 73

Weighted average cost of capital
     (WACC), 50
Wholesale funding, 59

Yield/beta ratio, 157
Yield curve, 39